MAR   2012

CULTURES OF THE WORLD

Thailand

Marshall Cavendish
Benchmark
New York

PICTURE CREDITS

Cover: © Jon Arnold Images/DanitaDelimont.com
Anders Blomqvist/Lonely Planet Images: 22 • Andrew Brownbill/Lonely Planet Images: 125 • Antony Giblin/
Lonely Planet Images: 96 • Ariadne Van Zandbergen/Lonely Planet Images: 32 • Athit Perawongmetha/Getty
Images: 34, 38 • Austin Bush/Lonely Planet Images: 58, 83, 89, 93, 126 • Brent Lewin/Bloomberg/Getty Images:
43 • Carol Wiley/Lonely Planet Images: 82, 101 • Chris Mellor/Lonely Planet Images: 15, 128 • Claver Carroll/
Lonely Planet Images: 116 • Dario Pignatelli/Bloomberg/Getty Images: 43 • Dennis Johnson/Lonely Planet
Images: 84 • Dominic Bonuccelli/Lonely Planet Images: 110 • Felix Hug/Lonely Planet Images: 108 • Inmagine.
com: 50, 52, 54, 61, 62, 63, 66, 71, 76, 80, 88, 112, 119, 120, 122, 130, 131 • Ira Block/National Geographic/
Getty Images: 109 • Jean-Pierre Lescourret/Lonely Planet Images: 9, 78 • Jerry Alexander/Lonely Planet Images:
73, 127 • Joe Cummings/Lonely Planet Images: 64, 103 • John Borthwick/Lonely Planet Images: 70, 92, 106,
117 • John Elk III/Lonely Planet Images: 10, 35, 124 • John Hay/Lonely Planet Images: 1 • Kraig Lieb/Lonely
Planet Images: 79, 102 • Kylie McLaughlin/Lonely Planet Images: 46, 99, 114 • Latitudestock/Getty Images:
27 • Madaree Tohlala/AFP/Getty Images: 51 • Manfred Gottschalk/Lonely Planet Images: 20 • Mick Elmore/
Lonely Planet Images: 3, 13, 18 • Oliver Strewe/Lonely Planet Images: 5 • Paul Beinssen/Lonely Planet Images:
23, 118 • Paula Bronstein/Liaison/Getty Images: 28 • Peter Stuckings/Lonely Planet Images: 40, 48 • Pornchai
Kittiwongsakul/AFP/Getty Images: 33 • Ray Laskowitz/Lonely Planet Images: 91 • Richard I'Anson/Lonely
Planet Images: 6, 75, 81, 100 • Saeed Khan/AFP/Getty Images • Tang Chhin Sothy/AFP/Getty Images: 29 •
Tom Cockrem/Lonely Planet Images: 41 • Udo Weitz/Bloomberg/Getty Images: 36

FRONT COVER

A young Thai girl drinking coconut juice at a roadside stall.

Publisher (U.S.): Michelle Bisson
Writers: Jim Goodman and Michael Spilling
Editors: Deborah Grahame-Smith, Stephanie Pee
Copyreader: Sherry Chiger
Designers: Nancy Sabato, Benson Tan
Cover picture researcher: Tracey Engel
Picture researcher: Joshua Ang

Marshall Cavendish Benchmark
99 White Plains Road
Tarrytown, NY 10591
Website: www.marshallcavendish.us

Library of Congress Cataloging-in-Publication Data
Goodman, Jim, 1947-
Thailand / Jim Goodman and Michael Spilling. — 3rd ed.
    p.cm. — (Cultures of the world)
  mary: Describes the geography, history, government, economy, people, religion, language, and culture of
  Thailand, a predominantly Buddhist country located in Southeast Asia. Includes several recipes.
Includes bibliographical references (p. 142) and index.
ISBN 978-1-60870-995-3 (print) — ISBN 978-0-7614-0002-8 (ebook)
1. Thailand—Juvenile literature. I. Spilling, Michael. II. Title.

DS563.5.G66 2013
959.3—dc23   2011042597

Printed in Malaysia
7 6 5 4 3 2 1

CONTENTS

THAILAND TODAY

KNOWN AS THE LAND OF SMILES, THAILAND ATTRACTS MILLIONS of tourists every year who return repeatedly to enjoy this amazing and exotic country. Visitors come to relax on its beautiful beaches, marvel at its ancient cities and temples, explore its mountains and jungles, and savor the special flavors of its cuisine.

United as a nation for almost 800 years, Thailand has a rich and colorful history, but the Thai people, now as in the past, are most proud of their independence. Thai trace their heritage to the country's ancient civilization and age-old traditions. In fact, Thailand is one of the largest and richest economies in Southeast Asia. Agriculture has always played an important part in Thailand's economy and the way of life of its rural people. It continues to do so today, although as a result of heavy foreign investment in the 1980s, Thailand's agricultural sector has been modernized and transformed.

Thai society today embraces this combination of modernity and progress while maintaining its distinctive identity. This attitude is demonstrated through the role

An aerial view of Bangkok's cityscape from the country's tallest building, Baiyoke Sky Tower.

of women in Thai society. Unlike other Asian cultures, Thailand has, in recent times, made great strides toward gender equality. Most women have considerable influence within the family, and some have achieved success in business and politics. An example of this is the appointment in July 2011 of Yingluck Shinawatra as Thailand's first female prime minister. While it would be true to say that many Thai women, particularly those from poorer backgrounds, continue to face discrimination and exploitation at home and in the workplace, many more educated women from the upper strata of society are beginning to wield power and respect. In Thailand today, it is possible to find women in top positions leading major corporations and public institutions. Even those from less wealthy backgrounds form a powerful mass of the urban workforce, working in places such as factories, food stalls, laundries, and beauty salons. The inequality gap between the sexes is narrowing, and with the recent historic appointment of the kingdom's first female prime minister, it is possible to see that in the near future, equality can be attained.

Living in modern Thailand can seem full of contradictions. The pace of life in bustling Bangkok, the capital city, is vibrant and chaotic. Life in urbanized Bangkok, sometimes known as the City of Angels, is akin to that of any major city in the West. Most visitors find Bangkok exciting but many of its more than 9.6 million residents bemoan the high cost of living, stifling pollution, and endless traffic jams. However, a short drive away from the intensity of Bangkok, it is still possible to find the tranquil charm of the countryside. It is this mixture of urban and rural, traditional and modern, that makes Thailand a unique country.

People commute by train, car, and buses, and in Bangkok there is also a subway and the Skytrain. In the big cities, the quality of life for the middle classes and the more affluent is generally good. In Bangkok and other major cities, well-off residents live in houses and condominiums, but on the other end of the spectrum, the less fortunate live in urban slums and shared accommodations with basic amenities. For those who can afford it, it is possible to live a Western lifestyle. For instance, there are supermarkets all over the country that carry Thai food as well as brands and items from the United States and Europe. Popular giant supermarkets include British-owned Tesco and French-owned Carrefour. Just as in many cities in the West, cell phones and cable and satellite television are available almost everywhere in addition to Internet connections. Cybercafes are also common in Thailand. DVD rentals are popular, as is going out to the movies, and many movie theaters have large screens and sophisticated sound systems. The big cities offer schools and hospitals of a very high standard.

Life for typical rural families can be quite different from that of people living in the cities. It is more common in rural areas for extended families with many generations to live together under the same roof or close to one another within the same compound. In the villages, where most houses are raised and built on poles, it is also typical to share living space with domestic animals such as chickens and buffalo. The animals are kept below while the family lives above. In such circumstances, privacy is rare although villagers, both young and old, enjoy the benefits of communal life.

Another attraction for visitors is the friendly and hospitable people of Thailand, many of whom have a wonderful and witty sense of humor. They are warm and welcoming to visitors but also generous and helpful toward each other. Many Thai believe that life should be enjoyed to the fullest. There is a real sense of community spirit among the Thai, and many go out of their way to support their friends, colleagues, and neighbors. This outlook starts early, and it is rare to encounter bullying or unkindness of any sort among Thai schoolchildren. Many Thai believe in respecting others and not infringing on their rights. Generally Thai adults as well as children are tolerant, mellow, and easygoing. The Thai value consensus, and so they often seem eager to please, tend to avoid any form of disagreement, and will make great efforts to avoid confrontation and preserve the peace. It seems that a Thai person would always choose harmony over conflict. This can be seen in the lack of tension and discord between the majority ethnic Chinese community and the various minority ethnic groups, including the Mon, the Khmer, the Burmese, the Lao, the Malays, the Indians, and the hill tribes.

However, there is an exception to their attitude of avoidance of conflict and confrontation in their political life. In recent years many Thai have been vociferously expressing their unhappiness with their government. For instance, in 2009 and 2010, antigovernment protestors in Bangkok clashed violently with authorities, resulting in the deaths of hundreds.

Thai people are particularly proud that theirs is the only country in South and Southeast Asia that has never been colonized by a foreign power. This has enabled them to forge a solid and individual culture. Although the Thai people have been exposed to a wide range of foreign influences over the years, they are still able to retain their sense of national identity.

There are two main beliefs that almost all Thai, young and old, share and that bind them together as a people. The first is their unquestioning loyalty, deep affection, and traditional reverence for the monarchy. The monarchy is considered sacred, and it is illegal to criticize this institution. To do so is deemed a serious and punishable offense with the possibility of imprisonment. This absolute reverence to the king sets Thailand apart from other monarchies in the world.

The second is their strong and unwavering faith in Buddhism. Even today in modern Thailand, Buddhism seeps into many aspects of everyday life. For instance, during the recent financial crises, many Thai turned to Buddhism for spiritual support in hard times. Their Buddhist beliefs are also a source of inspiration for many Thai artists, who draw upon their religion to create and develop sculpture, architecture, paintings, and literature.

Buddhist teachings have had a great influence in shaping the Thai character. For example, the concept of karma encourages the act of giving over wanting, allowing the individual to be more content with life. This may account for the strong sense of community among Thai and their fun-loving

Young novice monks taking a break. Buddhism is a great influence in Thailand, and many Thai males join Buddhist monastries in their youth.

and unselfish nature. Although the majority of Thai are Buddhists, almost all Thai, including Muslims, Christians, and the small percentage of Confucians, Taoists, and Hindus, live together amicably in present-day Thailand.

Religion plays a significant role in the life of a Thai person, but an increasing number of Thai are also taking an interest in and making time to care and express concern for their environment. Thailand has invested significantly in establishing an ecotourism industry so that it can offer the millions of visitors who come to the country every year an opportunity to appreciate its precious nature and culture without causing damage.

On the surface, Thailand seems to have rapidly and successfully developed from a mainly agricultural society to the impressive modern country it is today. However, it would be more accurate to describe Thailand as a country in transition that continues to uphold its traditional Eastern culture while offering its visitors and citizens a thoroughly modern way of life in terms of entertainment and leisure activities, such as sporting events, restaurants, and shopping. Possessing both the allure of the past and the excitement of modern attractions, Thailand is a country that has plenty to offer to its people and its visitors.

GEOGRAPHY

Thailand is home to gorgeous beaches, like this one at Ao Phante Malaka.

1

T HE KINGDOM OF THAILAND LIES at the southern part of the continent of Asia, in the heart of Southeast Asia. Thailand stretches 198,116 square miles (513,120 square km) between the 5° and 21° northern latitudes. The country's extreme dimensions are about 1,100 miles (1,770 km) from north to south and 500 miles (805 km) from east to west.

To the east and northeast, Thailand shares borders with Cambodia and Laos; to the northwest and west lies Myanmar (formerly Burma). Thailand's western peninsular provinces overlook the Andaman Sea, and the south is bounded by Malaysia. To the southeast is the Gulf of Thailand.

CLIMATE

Thailand's climate is hot and humid throughout the year. Average daily temperatures range from 68°F to 95°F (20°C—35°C). Average monthly rainfall ranges from 0.4 inches (10.2 mm) in January to 12 inches (305 mm) in September. Northern and central Thailand have three seasons: hot (March—June), rainy (June—October), and cooler (November—February). Southern Thailand has two seasons: dry (January—April) and rainy (May—December).

Situated in Southeast Asia, Thailand is almost equidistant from India and China.

BIRTH OF A NEW LAND

Some scientists believe that the land that is now Thailand began to take shape 60 million years ago when volcanoes to the south pushed the Indonesian island of Sumatra up against the Malay Peninsula, producing southern Thailand. About 35 million years later, what is now India collided into Asia, creating the mighty Himalayan Mountains and producing smaller ranges, such as those found on Thailand's western border.

Rising sea levels later filled low-lying areas around Southeast Asia. This formed the present-day Gulf of Thailand, a shallow sea with a mean depth of 148 feet (45 m) and a maximum depth of 262 feet (80 m), to the south of Thailand. The rising water also gave Thailand, the Malay Peninsula, and the Indonesian islands their current configurations. Sea levels reached their maximum height around 6,000 years ago when the shoreline of Thailand was 62 miles (100 km) farther inland than it is today. Much of the Chao Phraya Basin was underwater. Sea levels receded to their present levels approximately 5,500 years ago.

Most of Thailand's hills are made of granite, a hard volcanic rock, and limestone, a calcium-rich rock that dissolves readily. Thailand's contours are still changing. The formation of mountains continues, and there are occasional earthquakes. Along the Gulf of Thailand, storms sometimes produce waves up to 13 feet (4 m) high. These strong waves erode the coast, further changing the shape of the land.

MIXED NETWORK

Ancient Thai settlements were situated on rivers that served as channels of transportation and communication. Eventually people connected these rivers by means of canals, which now crisscross the heavily populated river basins.

The Thai first used boats of all kinds to bring goods and produce to markets and towns. Canals and rivers still play an important part today in the transportation of people and goods.

Thailand opened its first railway service in Bangkok in 1896, and by 1910 it had completed the tracks to Nakhon Ratchasima, a major town in the northeast. Railway and road construction, especially since World War II, has been effective in bringing skilled labor and construction materials to the provinces. This has improved the quality of provincial administrative services and the overall state of the economy.

According to 2006 estimates, there is a total of 111,880 miles (180,053 km) of roadways, including 280 miles (450 km) of expressways. Visitors to the capital city will be familiar with its infamous traffic chaos. To relieve traffic congestion, Bangkok built an elevated railway in 1999. Known as the Bangkok Mass Transit System or BTS Skytrain, it has two lines covering 14.2 miles (22.9 km) and more than 25 stations, and it transports approximately 450,000 passengers daily.

MAE NAM CHAO PHRAYA BASIN

The Mae Nam Chao Phraya Basin, also known as the Central Plains, is the country's most important rice-producing region as well as its most industrialized area. The area is fertile and contains approximately one-third of Thailand's population.

A traffic jam in Bangkok. Bangkok is notorious for its traffic congestion.

The Mae Nam Chao Phraya Basin is watered by three major rivers that flow from the north and join to form the Chao Phraya River at Nakhon Sawan. The Chao Phraya is the chief river of the Mae Nam Chao Phraya Basin. The Chao Phraya flows through the heart of Thailand, passing Bangkok en route to the sea. Although less than 231 miles (372 km) long, the Chao Phraya is one of the most important means of connecting Bangkok to the rest of the Central Plains. To the Thai, the Chao Phraya is the equivalent of Egypt's Nile River.

FLOATING MARKETS

In the mid-19th century, two-thirds of Bangkok's population lived in stilt houses along the banks of the Chao Phraya River. Food vendors used to sell their wares as they paddled their boats along Ratchaburi's crisscrossing canals. A bit of old Thailand survives just north of Bangkok at Damnoen Saduak. It is popularly known as the Floating Market.

Khlong (klohng) means "canal" in the Thai language; there are 83 canals in metropolitan Bangkok alone. Traversing these canals are many thousands of boats carrying all sorts of vegetables, fruit, dried fish, rice, flowers, and other products; some are floating kitchens—with food being cooked on small stoves—that sell ready-to-eat food such as noodles, fried bananas, fresh coconut milk, and desserts wrapped in banana leaves. The vendors usually finish selling their wares by late morning, before the food spoils in the heat of the afternoon sun.

The vendors are usually dressed in traditional dark-blue clothes and straw hats to ward off the sunlight. They load their boats before daybreak and paddle along the khlong *to the market. These vendors attach small oil lamps to their masts to light their way and as signals to other boats. Hundreds of these twinkling lamps assemble at the main market* khlong *every morning.*

The Mae Nam Chao Phraya Basin is also the site of several historical towns, including Lopburi, Nakhon Pathom, and the former capital of Ayutthaya. To the south and southeast of the basin lie the coastal areas and mineral-rich Chanthaburi; to the west lies Kanchanaburi, the most remote part of the country.

NORTHERN HILLS

The hills of Thailand's northernmost provinces are part of the Himalayas. Most of the hills have heights ranging from 3,300 to 6,600 feet (1,006–2,012 m). Towering over the northern mountains is Doi Inthanon, which at an elevation of 8,415 feet (2,565 m) is the tallest mountain in Thailand.

Traditional villages of Thailand's northern hill tribes nestle among the lush forest.

The Ping, Wang, Yom, Nan, and Pa Sak rivers flow among the mountains before eventually joining the Chao Phraya. The northern hills also have the greatest extremes in climate. During the cool season from November to February, night temperatures often fall below freezing. However, daytime temperatures in April and May can reach 104°F (40°C).

Dense tropical forests cover the hills. Small and spindly trees are common at lower elevations. Mosses, ferns, and creepers thrive in forests growing above 6,562 feet (2,000 m). The area is rich in history and culture. Some of the earliest Thai kingdoms originated here, in towns such as Chiang Saen, Chiang Rai, Chiang Mai, Phayao, and Nan. Ancient influences are evident in local architecture. Many of the houses in the northern hills are characterized by raised floors, slanting walls, and balconies.

ISAN

Thailand's northeastern provinces, known as Isan, lie on a limestone plateau bounded by the low but steep Phetchabun range to the west, the Dângrêk range along the Cambodian border to the south, and the Mekong River to the east. The plateau is not totally flat; depressions occur in some parts.

Bangkok is called the Venice of the East because of its numerous canals, although many have been drained, filled, and converted into much-needed streets. In the morning, the *khlong* are filled with all sorts of boats. There is only one rule: Vendors must try to leave the middle of the *khlong* open for boats to pass through. All too often, though, the narrow passageway gets clogged up as well. Then a special traffic policeman comes along on his boat and tries his best to untangle the mess.

THE GOLDEN TRIANGLE

The Golden Triangle in northern Thailand lies between Laos and Myanmar (formerly Burma). This notorious area was a leading center in Southeast Asia for the mass production of amphetamine (an addictive drug that increases people's energy), opium, and heroin until the 1980s.

Criminal drug organizations in Thailand produced opium and heroin from the milky latex of the seedpods of the poppy plant. Thai authorities have destroyed nearly all the poppy fields in the Golden Triangle and persuaded farmers to grow other crops. However, cultivation continues in remote areas across the Thai borders. Today it is possible to learn about the Golden Triangle's legacy and history by visiting two museums in the area. One is found right in Sop Ruak, while the newer and more extensive one, the Hall of Opium, is a little out of town.

Soils low in nutrients and poor irrigation characterize the region. The mountains form a barrier blocking the moist southerly winds. As a result, Isan receives little rainfall—about 47 inches (1,200 mm) a year—compared with the rest of Thailand. Isan is also prone to regular periods of drought.

Up to 80 percent of the total rainfall arrives during the monsoon period from mid-May to September, when rain falls almost every day. The continuous rain produces seasonal swamps in the depressions. Farmers grow rice in these areas. Where the soils are drier, farmers cultivate drought-resistant mulberry trees and harvest the leaves to feed silkworms. These worms spin silk that is exported to the United States and France, where fashion designers make expensive clothing with it. The Thai also weave the silk into beautiful cloth for their own clothing and dresses. The women carry baskets of silk cloth to towns such as Khon Kaen, where they sell the silk to tourists.

PENINSULAR THAILAND

The Bilauktaung range runs along the upper part of the Malay Peninsula, forming the border between Myanmar and Thailand. The Andaman Sea lies to the west of this narrow peninsula and the Gulf of Thailand to the east.

The climate in the south is less variable than in other parts of the nation. Temperatures are often as high as 91°F (33°C), with little variation each month. The peninsula receives up to 240 inches (6,096 mm) of rainfall every year.

Mountains of unusual shape—some rising to 5,000 feet (1,524 m)—line the Malay Peninsula. The Khao Luang, at 6,020 feet (1,835 m) above sea level, is the highest point of peninsular Thailand. Thick tropical forests cover the mountains. Beautiful islands, such as the Similan Islands, Koh Phi Phi, and Koh Samui, lie off either side of the peninsula and offer some of Asia's best beaches.

On the western side of the peninsula, next to the deep Andaman Sea, countless plantations grow rubber and oil palms. Tin deposits are found in the valleys and off the coast. The area along the Gulf of Thailand is devoted mostly to rice farming.

Except for Hat Yai, a shopping and entertainment center just north of the Malaysian border, the south's most important towns are all along the coasts: Pattani, Songkhla, Nakhon Si Thammarat, and Surat Thani on the gulf side and Ranong, Phuket, and Krabi on the Andaman side.

FLORA AND FAUNA

The climate of Thailand is warm and moist enough to support diverse rain forests and abundant animal life. Unfortunately development has diminished many of these natural assets.

FLORA Thailand boasts extensive wooded areas, with valuable trees such as teak, rosewood, and ebony. Evergreen species such as casuarina, a conifer with needle-shape leaves, and sappanwood, a tree producing yellow flowers and red sap, are found throughout the country. Thailand's fruit trees include banana, durian, mango, papaya, and jackfruit. In the rain-soaked peninsular jungles, you can find rattan palms and carnivorous plants such as the insect-eating pitcher plants. Mangroves, trees with roots that grow upward from the soil, occupy the swampy ground along tidal rivers, deltas, and coastlines in the south.

The 2,800-mile-long (4,506-km-long) Mekong River separates Myanmar from Laos immediately north of Thailand and then runs along the boundary between Thailand and Laos for 1,000 miles (1,609 km)—nearly the entire length of the Thai-Laotian border. With the reopening of Laos to trade and tourism, the Mekong is busier. Tourists to Laos often visit Isan as well. This has helped improve the Isan economy.

Kanchanaburi is Thailand's least populated province, full of lush jungles and thick forests, scenic rivers, and the country's most beautiful waterfalls.

In this region there stands a strange-looking bridge across the Meklang River. Meklang is also known as the Kwai Yai and is famous from the 1957 film The Bridge on the River Kwai. *During World War II, Japanese soldiers forced thousands of their Allied prisoners of war to construct a 258-mile-long (416-km-long) bridge on the river. In the process, an estimated 116,000 indigenous laborers and prisoners of war died because of physical abuse, starvation, disease, and exhaustion. Nearby, war graves mark the remains of nearly 7,000 Allied soldiers.*

Although the province attracts visitors, some are wary because of the presence of disease-carrying mosquitoes. Strangely, these mosquitoes have played an important role in preserving Kanchanaburi. The threat of brain fever and death resulting from mosquito bites discourages many people from going there.

There are many flowering shrubs and plants in Thailand. Among the most common and famous is the lotus, an aquatic plant that is rooted in mud but flowers above the water surface. Orchids grow wild in the jungles, and cultivated varieties thrive in nurseries, which are found mostly in the north. Other beautiful flowers include the small, yellow-white jasmine, a favorite offering at temples; the milky white frangipani; the bougainvillea; and the crimson hibiscus.

FAUNA Most of Thailand's wild animals live in dark, dense jungles. The Malayan tapir is one of the most unusual animals found in Thailand. It has a distinctive two-tone coloring; the front half of its body is black, and the rear half is mostly covered with white fur. The forests are also home to the boar, the porcupine, the monkey, the flying squirrel, and the endangered gibbon.

The jungles house a wide range of birds, species that eat insects and species that eat fruit and seeds. Pheasants are the most common birds in Thailand. Eagles and parakeets are less abundant. A large variety of insects populate the jungles of Thailand, including armored beetles and moths with wingspans of 12 inches (30 cm) or more.

Reptiles and amphibians thrive in Thailand's tropical climate. Many are dangerous, such as the cobra, the krait, and different kinds of vipers, as well as the crocodiles that live in rivers near the sea. The surrounding seas teem with fish and other marine life, such as crabs, lobsters, cockles, clams, and mussels, all of which often end up on Thai dinner tables.

INTERNET LINKS

www.mongabay.com/reference/country_studies/thailand/GEOGRAPHY.html

This website provides a useful overview of the geography of Thailand, including information on its boundaries, topography, drainage, regions, and climate.

www.nationsonline.org/oneworld/map/thailand_map2.htm

This website provides a detailed map showing Thailand and the surrounding countries, including the regions of Thailand, Bangkok and other major cities, expressways, and major airports.

www.wfft.org/

This is the official website of the Wildlife Friends Foundation Thailand (WFFT), an organization that aims to protect and conserve Thailand's wildlife and natural resources.

During the dry season, some Thai are known to rake through rubbish and fallen leaves in the areas surrounding houses in the countryside. They also light hundreds of bonfires. Are they preparing for an outdoor party? No, they are looking for snakes! The burning grass attracts snakes. People capture as many snakes as possible and sell them to snake farms. Poisonous snakes fetch the most money. Small snakes are fed to large ones.

HISTORY

The Khmer-style prang (corn cob-like structures found at temple grounds that usually housed important and sacred religious statues or relics) at the 12th-century Wat Phra Pai Luang in Sukhothai Historical Park. This was the location of Thailand's original capital.

2

HISTORIANS BELIEVE THAT HUNTER-gatherers were the first occupants of Thailand. These early peoples ate wild plants and hunted animals in the forests.

Archaeologists have uncovered pottery, stone tools, and fossilized seed fragments from edible plants in Mae Hong Son Province's Spirit Cave. Early societies probably left these remains behind 10,000 years ago. The Mekong River Valley and the Khorat Plateau were inhabited at this time, and rice was grown in the Khorat and Ban Prasat areas of northeastern Thailand as early as 4000 B.C. Mysterious rock paintings have been found in cliffs near the Thai-Laotian-Cambodian border as well as at Khao Kian in Phang Nga. Scientists know very little about the artists, except that they may have lived 3,000 years ago.

FIRST SETTLERS

The first genuine settlements—where people lived in groups, practiced agriculture, made pottery, and wove cloth—were established on hillsides. By 2000 B.C., there were several of these settlements throughout the country. Ban Chiang was one of the most important settlements. Scientists believe that the Ban Chiang settlement started developing around 3500 B.C. By 1000 B.C., outstanding ceramics were being produced. In Ban Chiang's later period, from 300 B.C. to A.D. 200, its craftsmen excelled in painted pottery, bronze and iron tools, and bronze and glass jewelry. These artifacts were buried with the dead.

MON, KHMER, AND INDIAN INFLUENCE

The first Indian immigrants to the Malay Peninsula began arriving in the third century B.C. According to historical records, they established 10 city-states around the time of Christ's birth and introduced Hinduism to the region. The most important of these city-states was Nakhon Si Thammarat, in the south of the country.

When the Mon, a people originally from southern China, migrated to the Mae Nam Chao Phraya Basin, they settled in inhabited areas and adopted Indian ideas of religion and handicraft. By the sixth century A.D., they had established the kingdom of Dvaravati at Nakhon Pathom. Later they expanded north to Haripunjaya (now Lamphun), south into the Malay Peninsula, and west into Burma (modern-day Myanmar), where they founded an important state at Pegu.

The Khmer, who were ethnically related to the Mon, expanded from their base in what is now Cambodia and settled in the Lower Mekong Valley. In a ninth-century war, they overpowered the Mon. Much of Thailand came

A detailed stone carving depicting a Hindu deity in the Khmer-style Phanom Rung temple.

under Khmer influence. Like the Mon, the Khmer adopted Indian customs and laws. The people believed the king had sacred powers bestowed by the local deities and by Hindu gods such as Indra, Vishnu, and Krishna. These gods protected the king and filled him with life-sustaining energy. His subjects worshipped him and paid him tributes of livestock and agricultural produce. The power of the Khmer peaked in the 11th century, when King Anawrahta (reigned 1044–77) of Burma pushed the Khmer eastward and briefly occupied the Central Plains. However, the Khmer still controlled much of Thailand through outposts at Lopburi and Phimai. They also controlled states in the south.

Ruins at the Sukhothai Historical Park, one of Thailand's heritage sites and also the original Thai capital.

EARLY THAI KINGDOMS

Groups of Thai began migrating into what is now Thailand from southern China perhaps as early as the eighth century A.D. The Shan were probably among the earliest Thai to enter the country. They spread from the mountains in northern and eastern Thailand to the lowland regions. These early Thai were skilled soldiers. Because of this, the Khmer began employing them as soldiers in the 12th century.

In 1238 Thai at Sukhothai refused to pay the customary tribute to their Khmer rulers, threw the Khmer out of the land, and established a new state. Sri Indraditya (reigned 1238–70) became leader. He was more like a father than a king to his people, more like a respected chieftain than an absolute ruler.

Under its greatest king, Ramkhamhaeng (reigned 1279–98), the Sukhothai kingdom conquered Khmer territory as far south as Nakhon Si Thammarat. This same monarch also created the Thai alphabet and encouraged an appreciation for the arts. His death in 1298 marked the decline of the Sukhothai empire. Around this time Thailand also started paying tribute to the Chinese emperors. Some historians believe this was the price for not being invaded by Kublai Khan's Mongol hordes, who had conquered China in the 13th century, and who also conquered parts of Burma and Vietnam.

First, the provinces around Sukhothai broke off all ties to the empire. Then the Mon of Pegu attacked and occupied part of the Malay Peninsula. Finally, a new state arose and, in 1378, invaded and conquered Sukhothai. This new state was the kingdom of Ayutthaya, which was founded in 1350 and soon became the mightiest of all Thai states. The kingdom was to have an unbroken, 400-year monarchy lasting 34 reigns, from Ramathibodi I (reigned 1350—69) to King Ekkathat (reigned 1758—67).

AYUTTHAYA

In the kingdom of Ayutthaya, also known as Siam, the king was an absolute monarch. A special royal language was used when speaking to the king or about the royal family.

The first king of Ayutthaya was Ramathibodi I, who was a warrior and a lawmaker. In fact, many of the laws he introduced were still in use in Thai society in the 19th century. The king distributed power and land to his subjects. The landholders had control over the workers on their plots. The king also ranked nobles of different grades and gave them titles according to how much land they had. Later, King Borommatrailokkanat (reigned 1448—88) set rules that determined how much land each noble could own.

The Ayutthaya kingdom fought many wars and conquered many territories during the first two centuries of its history. Having eliminated Sukhothai, the Siamese began conquering land in the south. Prisoners of war had to serve the Siamese as slaves. In 1431 King Boromaraja II (reigned 1424—48) destroyed the Khmer city of Angkor Thom, forcing the Khmer to retreat to Phnom Penh. This put an end to Khmer power in the region.

Nevertheless, Ayutthaya was no match for the Burmese who attacked Siam in 1549. Ayutthaya was subjugated in 1569, and Siam remained Burmese territory until 1584. In that year, Prince Naresuan (1555—1605), taking

In the 17th and 18th centuries, Ayutthaya was one of the wealthiest cities in Asia. In 1690 Engelbert Campfer, a Londoner visiting the city, proclaimed: "Among the Asian nations, the Kingdom of Siam is the greatest. The magnificence of the Ayutthaya Court is incomparable."

A GREEK IN THE COURT OF SIAM

Among the many adventurers who journeyed across Asia in the 17th century, one of the most memorable was an intrepid Greek sailor named Constantine Phaulkon (1647—88), also known as the Falcon of Siam.

As an employee of the British East India Company, Phaulkon caught the eye of King Narai during trade negotiations. Quick at mastering the Thai language as well as the nuances of court behavior, Phaulkon soon became a special adviser to the king. Under Phaulkon's guidance, Siam profited a great deal from its foreign trade with the Europeans.

Phaulkon was a Catholic, and he befriended the French Jesuits who came to Thailand. Through the Jesuits, the court of France tried to use Phaulkon's connection with the royal court of Thailand to spread the Catholic religion. The French wanted Phaulkon to persuade the king to become a Catholic. Phaulkon tried, but his efforts angered the Buddhist court so much that when Narai died, the next king immediately had Phaulkon beheaded and drove most of the Europeans out of the country.

advantage of a war in Burma, declared independence. Naresuan became king in 1590 and within three years drove the Burmese completely out of the region. He ruled over a vast area, including the land to the north and parts of Laos.

In the 17th century the kingdom of Ayutthaya was heavily involved with the West. Dutch merchants started trading in the south at Pattani in 1601, and English traders came to Ayutthaya in 1612. European rivalry for trade and port privileges peaked under Narai the Great (reigned 1656—88). The kingdom of Ayutthaya and the French king, Louis XIV, exchanged ambassadors. Narai trusted Europeans so much that he allowed them to join his court of ministers. After his death, the Siamese rebelled against the European presence. An internally weakened Siam was in no position then to defend itself, so the Burmese immediately took the opportunity to occupy the north. After one last period of stability for the kingdom under Borommakot (reigned 1732—58), Burmese soldiers put the capital of Ayutthaya to flames in 1767.

THE CHAKRI KINGS

Seven months later the Siamese general Phraya Taksin recaptured the city of Ayutthaya. Because the city had been destroyed, however, he decided to move the capital farther downriver to Thonburi, opposite modern-day Bangkok.

With the aid of two brothers, General Chao Phraya Chakri and General Chao Phraya Surasih, Taksin subdued fierce vassals, beat off another Burmese attack, and captured the north. Phraya Taksin was declared king in 1769. However, success eventually drove him insane, and he became extremely cruel. His generals removed him from the throne and executed him in 1782.

General Chao Phraya Chakri (reigned 1782—1809), better known by his royal title, Rama I, became the new king, establishing the Chakri Dynasty that still reigns today. Rama I moved the capital again, this time to Bangkok. He built the capital on the model of Ayutthaya. Under his care, Thai art and literature bloomed. Rama I supervised the construction of many magnificent buildings such as the Grand Palace and the Temple of the Emerald Buddha in Bangkok.

In 1818, beginning with a treaty with the Portuguese, Siam once again opened contacts with the West. Treaties were also negotiated with Britain in 1826 and the United States in 1833. These partnerships were generally aimed at obtaining favorable trading terms and privileges.

Meanwhile, Britain and France began colonizing Siam's neighbors, including territory that formerly belonged to Siam. At this critical point, Siam was blessed with outstanding rulers who were well versed in Western ways. They preserved the country's independence through reforms that modernized and strengthened the nation and ensured its independence in the face of expanding Western imperial ambitions.

The first of these kings was King Mongkut, or Rama IV (reigned 1851—68), a widely traveled former monk. He hired foreign tutors, including the English teacher Anna Leonowens, who arrived in Bangkok in 1862. Rama IV's successor, Chulalongkorn, ruled until 1910. He abolished slavery; improved national and local administration; hired foreign advisers to serve in his government; and developed railways, tramcars, and automobiles.

Under the rule of Rama VI (reigned 1910—25), Siam joined the Allies in World War I. With the Allied victory Siam signed the Treaty of Versailles, a formal recognition of Siam's status as a member of the League of Nations, which had been set up in 1919 to promote international cooperation and peace. As a member, Siam gained prestige and power internationally. Rama VI also made Siam the first country in Asia with compulsory education.

THE 1932 REVOLUTION

Despite the progress the kings brought the nation, the Thai people began to think that an absolute monarchy was a barrier to further growth. In the early 1930s, the Great Depression created financial problems for the Thai economy. The king tried to solve this by taxing salaries. The move only made the Thai more dissatisfied with the monarchy. In 1932 a group of army officers and intellectuals overthrew the royal government in a bloodless revolution.

A statue of King Mongkut at the Wat Phra Keaw, located within the confines of the Royal Palace.

The new rulers announced the beginning of a constitutional monarchy similar to the British model, but with a mixed military-civilian group in power. They immediately expanded elementary education, improved the administration of the nation, and changed the country's name from Siam to Thailand, "Land of the Free."

In 1935 the king, Rama VII, abdicated without naming a successor. The cabinet promoted his 10-year-old nephew, Ananda Mahidol, to the throne as Rama VIII, although he remained at school in Switzerland until the end of World War II in 1945. Phibun Songkhram, a key military leader in the 1932 coup, led the country from 1938 until 1944. Between 1932 and 1992 Thailand was to suffer 18 attempted coups.

DEMOCRACY AND MILITARY RULE

After Marshal Phibun Songkhram assumed power in 1938, he demanded that France return the parts of Laos and Cambodia that formerly belonged to Siam.

When the French refused to comply, fighting broke out. In May 1941, with the help of Japan, the Thai and Indo-French authorities resolved the issue by signing the Tokyo Convention. France returned Battambong, Champasak, Lanchang, and Siamrap to Thailand.

As an ally of Japan in World War II, the Thai government declared war on the United States. But Thailand's ambassador in Washington refused to deliver the declaration, stating that it did not represent the people's will. The United States said it did not recognize the declaration anyway.

Tragedy marked the immediate postwar period when Ananda Mahidol, King Rama VIII, was mysteriously assassinated in 1946. He was succeeded by King Bhumibol, or Rama IX. The government fell when the army, playing the role of the "protector of the nation," staged a coup. Phibun Songkhram returned to power for 10 years until another military coup ousted him.

From 1964 to 1973 the Thai nation was ruled by Field Marshal Thanom Kittikachorn and General Praphat Charusathien. The new government promoted investment. The friendly ties Thailand and the United States maintained during the Vietnam War, when the United States used air bases in Thailand, also boosted economic growth in the 1960s and 1970s. The increasing wealth of the nation gave more power and confidence to the middle class, which began to be dissatisfied with military rule.

In October 1973 a group of students led a civilian revolt against the military regime. When the army refused to obey government orders and the king indicated that he too favored a change, the government resigned. Thailand now turned toward socialism. Many students supported farmer and labor movements. When the communists became powerful in neighboring Vietnam, Laos, and Cambodia, Thailand's government requested that

Students from Ramkamhaeng University protesting at a demonstration denouncing General Suchinda in 1992.

the United States close down its military bases in the country because it did not want any trouble with neighboring Vietnam.

In 1980 General Prem Tinsulanonda took power. He governed for eight years, overseeing rapid economic development and bringing about peace and the decline of socialism. After his retirement, Thai politics entered an unstable period. Top military officers attempted to wield power against the wishes of the growing and increasingly articulate middle class, which desired greater democracy. This tension led to a violent confrontation in May 1992, in which scores of demonstrators in Bangkok were killed. In the aftermath, elections were held. The pro-military parties lost, and a new coalition gained power under Prime Minister Chuan Leekpai.

Meanwhile, the highly popular King Bhumibol remained monarch. Beyond his ceremonial role, he frequently visited the provinces and sponsored development programs. It was largely due to his personal intervention that the violent political crisis of 1992 was defused.

Former Thai prime minister Thaksin Shinawatra.

MODERN HISTORY

In 2001 the populist Thai Rak Thai (TRT) party, led by Prime Minister Thaksin Shinawatra, came to power. Thaksin was popular with the rural and urban poor for introducing social programs. However, his rule was much less popular with the urban middle class and the wealthy, because he destroyed the country's financial stability. Thaksin was challenged by Sondhi Limthongkul, a well-known media tycoon, who developed an alternative mass protest movement under the name of the People's Alliance for Democracy (PAD).

In 2006, while Thaksin was at a United Nations meeting in New York, the commander in chief of the Royal Thai Army, General Sonthi Boonyaratglin,

INSURGENCY IN THE SOUTH

In Thailand's southern provinces of Pattani, Narathiwat, and Yala, an antigovernment insurgency has been raging for many decades. Since 2004 the number of violent attacks on government targets has dramatically increased, with almost 4,000 people thought to have died. Police stations and schools have been bombed and government employees targeted in shootings. Tens of thousands of Thai troops have been deployed to try to control the violence.

The causes of the rebellion are many: The Thai in these southern provinces are mainly Muslim, with many cultural links to Muslim Malaysia to the south. They claim that the Thai authorities are insensitive to their culture and values. One unusual aspect of the insurgency is that no one group or leader has been identified to represent the movement and that few concrete demands have been made, other than the right to use the Yawi language, the local dialect very similar to Malay.

The rebellion has divided southern Thai mainly along religious lines, with many Buddhist Thai arming themselves for self-protection. Muslim targets have also been attacked by Buddhist vigilantes.

Observers believe that the insurgency has little to do with global jihadism and that the various groups in southern Thailand have little or no contact with regional or international terrorist organizations such as Jemaah Islamiyah, which was responsible for the Bali bombings in 2002. It seems that the southern Malay Thai just want more freedom and control over their local affairs. Abhisit's government had taken a conciliatory tone toward the insurgency, but the violence has divided local communities, and trust needs to be rebuilt before peace can be restored.

led a bloodless coup supported by many elements of the opposition. A general election in December 2007 restored a civilian government, led by Samak Sundaravej of the People's Power Party (PPP), a descendant of the TRT. In mid-2008 the PAD led massive street demonstrations against Samak Sundaravej's government, which it criticized for his connections with the exiled former prime minister Thaksin Shinawatra. Somchai Wongsawat, also of the PPP, replaced Samak Sundaravej as prime minster.

Thaksin supporters responded with their own counterdemonstrations, while PAD supporters occupied both major airports for a week. In December 2008 the Constitutional Court of Thailand removed Somchai Wongsawat from office. Following a parliamentary vote, Abhisit Vejjajiva was appointed the country's 27th prime minister.

In 2009 and 2010 Thailand was the scene of further protests and crackdowns, with protesters erecting barricades on the streets of Bangkok. Hundreds of people are estimated to have died in the violence. However, although Abhisit's government introduced policies aimed at alleviating rural poverty and improving the country's infrastructure, the political landscape remained uncertain in the face of the global recession of 2008-2010.

In the most recent parliamentary elections, in July 2011, Pheu Thai, an opposition party led by Yingluck Shinawatra, sister of Thaksin Shinawatra, won an overall majority. Abhisit Vejjajiva's Democrat Party came second. Yingluck Shinawatra is Thailand's first female prime minister. Like her brother, Yingluck had campaigned on a platform of policies to improve the lot of the rural poor, and her victory was seen as a rebuke to the traditional political elite—the urban rich and the army generals.

INTERNET LINKS

http://whc.unesco.org/en/list/576

This UNESCO website offers descriptions, maps, and photographs of Thailand's ancient capital, Ayutthaya.

www.lonelyplanet.com/thailand/history

This well-known travel site offers a clear and concise overview of the history of Thailand from prehistory to the present.

www.soravij.com/kings.html

This website provides descriptions and photographs of all the Thai kings of the Chakri Dynasty.

GOVERNMENT

The Dusit Maha Prasat throne hall in the Grand Palace.

3

THE 1978 CONSTITUTION STATES that the king is the head of the state, and his sovereign power comes from the people. Under the constitutional monarchy, the king exercises his power through the National Assembly.

The National Assembly of Thailand is a bicameral (two-house) legislature consisting of the Senate and the House of Representatives. The legislative branch took its current form in 2007 following the newly drafted constitution of that year. The National Assembly has 630 members. Both houses of the National Assembly meet at the Parliament House of Thailand.

Thailand is a constitutional monarchy. The current monarch, King Rama IX of the Chakri Dynasty, has reigned since 1946, making him the longest-serving head of state in the world today and the longest-reigning monarch in Thai history.

Members of the Thai National Assembly awaiting Prime Minister Yingluck Shinawatra's inaugural address in 2011.

The current Senate has 150 members. Each of the country's 75 provinces and the municipality of Bangkok elect one member; the other 74 members are selected by the Senate Selection Commission, made up of both elected and appointed officials. The House of Representatives is made up of 480 members; 400 are directly elected from constituencies around the country in democratic elections, whereas the other 80 members are selected using "proportional representation" through party lists.

However, real power belongs to the prime minister. The prime minister's office makes national policies and manages several financial and development offices. The prime minister is usually the leader of the party that wins the most seats in the parliamentary elections. He or she is also the chairman of the cabinet, called the Council of Ministers, which consists of 35 ministers from the prime minister's party and the governing coalition. The most important of these are the ministers of defense, finance, and the interior.

Members of the National Assembly and the Council of Ministers may propose laws. Each minister—with one or two deputies and one appointed secretary—runs several departments that oversee the operations of divisions and subsections.

Thai Prime Minister Yingluck Shinawatra is the country's first female prime minister.

PROVINCES

Thailand has 75 provinces, each with its own governor who has to report to the Ministry of the Interior. Officials trained in the capital usually fill higher administrative positions in each province. Officials trained in the provinces are usually employed at lower administrative levels.

The Ministry of the Interior is the country's largest and most important ministry. It is in charge of public land and forest reservations and oversees domestic affairs: public works, rural development, town and country planning, community development, labor matters, and law and order.

VILLAGES

When King Chulalongkorn improved provincial administration, the rural population in existing villages was organized into *muban* (MOO-bahn), which means "clusters of houses." This is still the system today. Moreover, 10 to 15 *muban*, or administrative villages, make up one *tambon* (TAM-bohn). In 2008 there were 74,944 *muban* in Thailand.

Each village elects its own headman, who acts as its representative when dealing with the government. Village heads serve for five-year terms but can seek reelection. For most Thai villages in the lowlands, this has always been the practice. When the hill people became a part of Thailand, they had to adapt their traditions to suit the lowland customs. Usually the group chooses someone as headman who is fluent in Thai, so that he can easily

Aerial view of a village in the Doi Ang Khang region of Chiang Mai.

communicate with the government. He is usually one of the most respected, industrious, and prosperous members of the community and a person of good moral character.

Children used to go to school in the local temple compound. Now schools are set up outside temples, and the school curriculum provides standardized secular education.

The village regards its schoolteachers as important people. Teachers explain the world of politics and related matters to the villagers. The Thai take teachers' opinions on local problems and national affairs very seriously. Teachers have to obtain a certificate from a teachers' training school before they are qualified to teach. Not every village has a training school. People who want to be teachers often have to travel to nearby towns for training.

UPHOLDING THE LAW

The judiciary is divided into three distinct systems: the Court of Justice, the Administrative Court, and the Constitutional Court of Thailand. Legal cases in Thailand fall under one of the following areas: labor, tax, family, juvenile,

A hearing in Thailand's Supreme Court.

military, civil, or criminal. Those who are arrested are held in police stations. Charges against them must be filed within three days for minor offenses and within seven for felonies.

After that, the police will send the prosecutor a summary of the evidence of the crime, along with some recommendations. The prosecutor then decides the nature of the charge and whether it should be dropped or if bail should be granted. Bail is set according to the charge and the fines. There is no jury system in Thailand; the judge decides everything. Appeals may be made, in writing only, to the Court of Appeals or the Supreme Court, based on the severity of the crime. Appeals must be filed within 30 days of the judge's reading, signing, and issuing the verdict. Sentences are usually very heavy. Except for drug and security offenses and slander of or insults to the royal family, annual royal pardons reduce the time served.

To become an attorney, a student must pass the bar examination. After three years of practice, the attorney may take another examination to become a judge or a prosecutor. He or she is then eligible for promotion to various levels in the national judicial department.

THE ARMY

The Royal Thai Armed Forces were created in 1852 by King Mongkut, who needed a European-trained military force to thwart any attempts at colonization. Today there are more than 800,000 personnel in the Royal Thai Armed Forces. Potential military officers spend the first two years of service at a military academy. After this, they can choose their area of service and attend the appropriate academy for four years.

Since World War II, the military's primary defense activities have been focused on breaking up the communist movement—primarily in the northeast—and fighting a Muslim separatist campaign in the south. During the Indo-French wars, the military had to guard the border with Laos and Cambodia. More recently, the Myanmar frontier has become a hot zone as the war in Myanmar between the army and various ethnic groups occasionally spills into Thai territory. Thailand has also been involved in territorial

Since 1932 Thailand has been a constitutional monarchy—that is, the king is the head of state, but the power of the state is held by a democratically elected parliament. The current king of Thailand, King Bhumibol Adulyadej, or Rama IX, has reigned since 1946, making him the world's longest-reigning monarch. Under the 1924 Law of Palace Succession, kingship passes down the male line, from father to son. The current heir to the throne is the crown prince of Thailand, Prince Maha Vajiralongkorn. Although the king has very little direct power as the head of state, he commands enormous popular respect and moral authority. According to the constitution, the king is head of the armed forces, and he has to be a Buddhist as well as the defender of all religious faiths in the country.

The king and the royal family are highly respected in Thailand, both as a figurehead of the Thai nation and as a mediator in times of strife. Insulting the king and the institution of the monarchy can result in heavy punishments. In 1992 Bhumibol played a key role in Thailand's transition to a democratic system, helping avert civil war by making a televised appeal to the various groups to find a peaceful solution to the conflict. Bhumibol also helped resolve the political crisis of 2006.

The monarchy's official residence is the Grand Palace in Bangkok. However, the current king spends most of his time at the Chitralada Palace, also in Bangkok, and the Klai Kangwon Palace in Hua Hin.

disputes with its eastern neighbors, especially Cambodia. In 2010 shots were exchanged on the Thai-Cambodian border, with casualties on both sides.

Special military units patrol parts of Thailand's border. In the north these units, along with the Border Patrol Police, are involved in the location and destruction of opium fields and heroin factories, as well as in the fight against amphetamine smuggling.

Thailand's middle class has little sympathy for military interference in politics. After the 1992 uprising against General Suchinda Kraprayoon, the discredited political parties that supported the military government lost the next election. Since then, the government has taken measures to reduce the army's political influence. Likewise, the nation's military commanders insist on maintaining a neutral attitude toward any elected government by not backing any one political party in the elections. Following the political turmoil of 2006 the army played a role in drafting and upholding the 2007 constitution.

INTERNET LINKS

http://countrystudies.us/thailand/78.htm

This website provides a detailed history and description of local government in Thailand.

http://thailand-usa.com/law-ethics/thai-parliament-national-assembly/

This information portal and community hub offers a broad range of information related to Thailand and the United States. The site also allows you to compare the Thai National Assembly with the U.S. Congress.

www.soravij.com/rama9.html

This website is dedicated to King Bhumibol Adulyadej (Rama IX). It includes a history of Rama IX and the Chakri Dynasty with photographs.

www.statoids.com/uth.html

This website offers statistics on all of Thailand's provinces, from 1947 to the present.

ECONOMY

A young Thai girl walks through a tea plantation.

4

N 2010 THAILAND HAD THE SECOND-largest economy in Southeast Asia (after the highly populous Indonesia) and the 24th largest in the world. In terms of per capita (per person) wealth, Thailand is the fourth richest in Southeast Asia, after Singapore, Brunei, and Malaysia.

Before King Mongkut opened the country's doors to the West, Thailand's economy was almost completely dependent on agriculture, and people made little use of other resources. The Thai economy began to grow after 1957 when the government decided to encourage investment.

Thailand is a newly industrialized economy, reliant on exports of things such as auto parts and electronic goods and a rapidly expanding tourist sector.

Farmland overlooking a river and mountains in Thailand's Mae Hong Son province.

That resulted in the establishment of new firms and development in many areas. In 1959 the creation of the Board of Investment persuaded foreign firms to set up international business branches in Thailand. Japan and the United States are among Thailand's largest investors.

In the 10 years up to 1995 Thailand had one of the world's fastest-growing economies, at an average rate of 8—9 percent a year. However, continued growth and prosperity in the 1990s concealed structural weaknesses in the Thai economy, especially in the financial sector. New wealth was largely based on property speculation, rather than on the sale of goods. Many Thai borrowed money from banks and finance companies to pay for the development and construction of buildings. In turn, Thai banks and companies borrowed recklessly from foreign banks. They often could not repay the foreign banks or recover their loans.

In 1997 the Thai baht fell suddenly, triggering the Asian currency crisis. Unemployment rose, and investment all but halted. In 1999 with the aid of the International Monetary Fund, Thailand began drastic reforms in banking and finance. In the first decade of the 21st century, the Thai economy grew rapidly, although it suffered from the world economic downturn of 2008—2010. In 2011 the World Bank predicted that the Thai economy would grow by 3.7 percent—a low figure by the standards of other Asian economies but solid growth nonetheless. Unemployment was at a very low 1.6 percent in 2011 and predicted to remain low in a country where foreign investment was strong and consumer confidence high.

TOWARD A MODERN ECONOMY

The country's growth has mainly been reflected in the development of its industries and services. In the 1960s most processed goods were imported, including the food items that filled the shelves of shops in small towns and villages. Today many products previously imported—from food items to automobiles and vehicle parts—are made in Thailand. The modern Thai economy is heavily reliant on exports, with two-thirds of the country's earnings coming from exported goods such as cars, auto parts, computers, clothing, and electronic goods. In 2010 Thailand produced 1.6 million cars, and it is predicted that by 2015 it will be one of the top 10 carmakers in the world. The United States is the main destination for Thailand's exports, followed by China, Japan, and Thailand's regional neighbors.

The growth in trade has been matched by an improvement in transportation services—new roads, buses, and trucks. Construction also has boomed since the 1960s, giving rise to new office and apartment buildings.

What's more, there has been an expansion of markets, from the ordinary weekend markets in rural areas to the fancy, multilevel shopping malls in Bangkok, marking the emergence of a consumer society. Small-scale enterprises flourish in Thailand. Today every town has its own night market, featuring the products of individual and family businesses.

While economic development has touched every part of the country, Bangkok is still the place to make a fortune. Bangkok is not merely Thailand's banking capital but also, along with Hong Kong and Singapore, one of the leading financial centers in Southeast Asia.

However, the benefits of Thailand's economic progress have not been shared equally, with some regions—particularly the north and the northeast—struggling to reduce poverty at the same rate as Bangkok and the wealthy tourist areas of the south.

A factory worker at a chemical factory works on a wool-combing machine.

FARMING

Almost half of Thailand's population is engaged in some form of agricultural work, although the sector accounts for just 10 percent of the country's economy. In the food industry Thailand has long been known as the Kitchen of the World, not only from its wealth of spices but also because it's the world's biggest rice exporter. In recent decades, however, rice has become much less important to the Thai economy. In 1950 rice accounted for half of the total exports; by 1984 the percentage had dropped to 15 percent. Currently the average yields of Thai rice in one unit area of land are among the lowest in Asia.

Other important agricultural sectors include fish products, grain, and rubber. Although the tsunami of December 2004 devastated the Thai fishing industry, today Thailand leads the world in the export of black tiger prawns. The country is the largest regional producer of chicken.

Agricultural development has not been encouraged in the same way as development in the industrial sector, but reservoirs and irrigation channels to rivers have been built to help farmers. In addition, more than 1,000 royally sponsored, small-scale rural projects have been set up to help the agricultural economy. Although Thailand has modern farming equipment such as tractors and motorized plows, most farmers still perform heavy labor manually. Development efforts in the farm sector are directed toward increasing grain production. Moreover, while farms do not suffer from a shortage of labor in Thailand, poor soil and irregular rainfall patterns hinder the growth of the agricultural sector of the Thai economy.

The soil in the hills is difficult to farm because of the uneven ground. Still, the hilly areas of Thailand are important to the economy. Farmers cultivate cool-weather fruits such as peaches and nectarines in the northern hills for sale in nearby cities such as Chiang Mai and Chiang Rai. The commercial logging industry obtains most of its income from the trees in the forested hills.

TOURISM

Besides foreign investment and earnings from exports, Thailand's economy has been boosted by the incredible rise in tourism. Tourism makes a larger contribution to Thailand's economy than to that of any other Asian nation.

In 2010 some 15 million tourists visited Thailand, after steady growth throughout the decade. Tourists from other Asian countries, such as Malaysia, China, and Japan, make up the majority of tourists, although large numbers of Europeans, North Americans, and Australians also go there. Most come for relaxation, especially to Thailand's many beach resorts and dive sites, such as Phuket, Krabi, and Koh Samui. Cultural and historical attractions in Bangkok, Ayutthaya, and Chiang Mai are also major pulls.

Tourism revenue in 1991 totaled 100 billion baht, making it more valuable than the exports of textiles, rice, rubber, and tapioca combined. Tourism revenue had risen to 290 billion baht by 2000 and 547 billion baht in 2007.

Growth in tourism has encouraged businesses in the service sector that are directly connected to tourism. These include the hotel, restaurant, and travel industries. The tourism boost has also restarted the handicraft business. Weavers, embroiderers, carvers, goldsmiths, and other artisans are turning out all kinds of traditional craft items to sell as tourist souvenirs. In doing so, these artisans preserve ancient skills that might otherwise quietly die out.

Tourists at a shopping mall in Bangkok. Thailand's rich culture, diverse flora and fauna, and beautiful beaches and dive sites attract millions of tourists every year.

THAILAND FLOODS

In 2011, the monsoon season brought an unusually high volume of rainfall to Thailand, in particular northern Thailand. This in turn caused many rivers (the Chao Phraya as well as the Mekong and its tributaries) to swell and breach their banks, flooding many of the lower lying provinces in Thailand. As the water drained from the higher elevations in the north to the lower lying areas in the south (toward the Ayuttaya Sea), Bangkok was in danger of flooding and the government scrambled to find means to keep the capital city dry, building barriers along the riverbank and also around factories integral to both the country's economy and global manufacturing supply chains.

Unfortunately, the volume of water was too great for the barriers to handle and industrial estates were flooded and important services like power plants and hospitals were halted.

The repercussions of the flood were far-reaching. Many of the factories that were submerged by the floodwaters produced essential parts for some of the biggest automotive and technological companies. Thailand is the world's second-largest producer of hard-disks and the loss in production drove prices of hard-disks up and many of the affected companies have reported and projected losses due to the floods.

Thailand also accounts for about 30 percent of the world trade in rice and with crops devastated by the floods, the price of rice was expected to increase. The floods also impacted Thailand's robust tourism industry, with fewer tourists visiting the country. There was also concern over disease and sanitation and people were advised to keep out of the water.

The floods caused divisions within the Thai community as well. People questioned if the flood could have been better managed and many residents of Bangkok were angry at the government's decision to "sacrifice" certain parts of Bangkok (by allowing it to flood) to protect other sections. Some citizens destroyed certain sections of the flood barrier to show their discontent.

VANISHING OCCUPATIONS

In the modern Thai economy, many time-honored occupations have been lost. Some have been replaced by more-efficient techniques; others have been abandoned because of changes in available materials or in consumer demand. Among the occupations disappearing from the scene are the itinerant dyer, the boat and truck illustrator, the lute player, and the makers of monks' wooden begging bowls, theatrical masks and puppets, and granite mortars and pestles. Working elephants are also becoming a thing of the past.

INTERNET LINKS

www.bbc.co.uk/learningzone/clips/working-in-the-thai-rice-industry/11366.html

This website features a BBC film that shows British students learning how Thai farmers pick rice.

www.chiangmai-chiangrai.com/thailand-textile-industry.html

This website provides shows how textiles are produced in the north of Thailand.

www.elephantnaturefoundation.org/

The Elephant Nature Foundation is a charitable organization that supports the rights of elephants in Thailand. Its website includes articles, links, and photographs.

www.worldbank.or.th

This website provides the World Bank's latest report on the Thai economy, summarized in easy-to-understand points, with numerous links to more-detailed analysis.

ENVIRONMENT

Tourists on an elephant trek in Ban Ruammit.
Thailand is home to beautiful beaches and lush forests.

5

T HAILAND'S FIELDS AND FORESTS are home to more than 1,500 kinds of trees, 800 types of ferns, and 27,000 types of flowers—10 percent of the world's total—including 1,300 types of orchids, the greatest variety anywhere. The country's animals include 282 mammal, 925 bird, and 176 snake species.

Many animals, however, such as tigers, gibbons, and rhinoceros hornbills, are close to extinction in the country. Thailand has 15 protected animals that it is illegal to hunt, breed, or trade. These include the Javan and Sumatran rhinoceroses, the wild Asian water buffalo, the Malayan tapir, and the coastal-dwelling dugong. Wildlife is largely confined to national parks and the jungles of Kanchanaburi and western Thailand. In the rush to modernize and enrich the nation, developers paid little attention to the environmental impact of their projects: Large tracts of forest disappeared beneath the axes of logging companies; fishing with dynamite destroyed exquisite coral reefs; the extension of prawn farms ruined adjacent cropland; and waste products from mines, factories, and industrial plants contaminated rivers.

THE PROBLEM WITH PRAWNS

In recent decades the creation of prawn farms has brought increased incomes to fishermen along Thailand's peninsular coastlines. This business has developed rapidly; the number of prawn farms increased

A prawn farm on the outskirts of Bangkok.

from 4,544 in 1985 to 15,060 in 1990. Thailand today has more than 30,000 prawn farms. Most are located in the southern provinces such as Surat Thani, well away from busy industrial centers.

Big companies are now buying out smaller enterprises and are using chemicals to feed the prawns and to fortify the breeding grounds against disease. Often the strong chemicals used in prawn farms destroyed the original breeding grounds. The chemicals sometimes leaked into coastal swamps and polluted mangrove forests. Due to pollution from prawn farming, most of the mangrove forests along the eastern and western coasts facing the Gulf of Thailand have disappeared. In recent years, the Thai government has introduced strict regulations to make sure that the prawn farms produce prawns fit for the international market.

Black tiger prawns are one of the most highly sought-after species in Thailand. This species lives only in brackish water. To breed black tiger prawns, farmers have to use large amounts of seawater in their farms. As a result, the land around the prawn farms becomes salty and less fertile.

"Man, forest, and wildlife are mutually interrelated and therefore inseparable."
—Queen Sirikit

Prawn-farming companies have tried to move inland, but they face strong local and national opposition. In 1998 the National Environmental Board banned inland prawn farming in eight provinces around Bangkok in the Central Plains, where most of Thailand's rice is cultivated. In 2001 the companies attempted to have the ban lifted but were stopped by King Bhumibol.

SHRINKING FORESTS

Between 1945 and 1975 forests in Thailand were reduced from 61 percent of the total land to 34 percent of the land area—that is, Thailand lost more than a third of its forests in this 30-year period. During the next decade almost 28 percent of the remaining forests were also lost to logging practices and land being cleared for agriculture. Teak has long been the most profitable of the desirable tropical woods from Thailand, and even as late as 1988, teak generated $20 million in revenue, despite a ban in 1973 of exports of teakwood.

Loss of forest cover has increased the incidence of landslides in Thailand, especially after torrential rain.

Despite the government's efforts to maintain forest cover, illegal logging is still rampant in Thailand.

Between November 19 and 24, 1988, heavy rains triggered massive landslides that affected 16 villages in southern Thailand. Three villages were buried under 3—10 feet (1—3 m) of sand and debris. The severe floods also caused the deaths of 373 people, as well as injuring hundreds of others. The landslides were blamed on deforestation, which had weakened forest soil. As a consequence, in 1989 the government introduced a logging ban by revoking all logging concessions. In 1991 the government revised its policy to maintain a 40 percent forest cover target—25 percent conservation forest and 15 percent production forest.

However, illegal logging has continued ever since. The business is very lucrative, for both the logging "barons" who control the business and the many corrupt local officials who gain from the illegal logging trade. Furthermore, villagers in some parts of Thailand have come to rely on logging as their main source of income. By 1999 just 25 percent of Thailand was virgin forest. Despite the legislation, it is estimated that between 1990 and 2005, Thailand lost an additional 9 percent of its forest cover, or about 3.46 million acres (1.4 million ha).

BRING BACK THE FOREST

In places such as Dong Yai, in northeastern Thailand, loggers are granted concessions only if they promise to replant trees in the areas they clear. In many cases, the loggers plant only eucalyptus, which they can harvest in two to three years. Eucalyptus absorbs all the nutrients in the soil to support its fast growth, after which nothing else can grow there. In recent years environmentally conscious nongovernmental organizations (NGOs) have been trying to persuade loggers to plant other trees in their reforestation programs. Whether the NGOs succeed in significantly expanding the forest cover, though, will depend on whether the government can be persuaded to make environmental protection a greater priority than economic development.

How does one bring back a forest to a patch of abandoned, degraded land? The Forest Restoration Research Unit (FORRU), headquartered in Chiang Mai University, has already begun answering that question through a project in northern Thailand. FORRU's method is to first study the properties of the various species of trees native to northern Thailand, to determine which will be best at reestablishing the forest.

Then, FORRU plants several desirable tree species at once. Rapidly growing pioneer trees form a canopy that attracts birds, the principal seed dispersers now that the big mammals are all but extinct. A secondary forest soon develops. Species such as fig and hog plum produce fruits that attract small mammals such as squirrels and civets.

Primary tree species grow at a slower pace. They start life under the pioneer tree species. When after 10—25 years the original pioneer trees die, the primary trees form a new canopy. The secondary forest then starts to resemble a primary forest.

Despite the continued depletion of Thai forests, wood products remain a major Thai export. Consequently Thailand has become a net importer of timber from neighboring countries, especially Myanmar and Laos. Timber is brought in from these countries, turned into wood products, and then exported for sale. If the practice continues at its current pace, then one of the world's great teak forests could disappear entirely across all of these countries.

A family using face masks to protect themselves from air pollution, which can have serious health repercussions.

SMOKE IN THE CITIES

Emissions from industrial plants and vehicles contaminate the atmosphere in cities, creating newer health hazards for residents. Small particles of carbon from smokestacks and exhaust pipes fill the air, causing lung and other respiratory ailments. Smoke irritates the eyes and can lead to a breakdown of the nervous system and even cancer. The use of diesel fuel and low-grade lubricating oil reduces fuel-use efficiency, which further complicates the problem by releasing carbon monoxide into the air. This colorless, odorless gas damages the brain and arteries and, in large doses, causes death.

Pollutants in the air collect on the surface of food cooked outdoors. These pollutants contaminate the food and harm the digestive system. People living in the cities often fall ill after consuming food from open-air restaurants and street vendors.

In the 1990s the government began taking steps to deal with the adverse environmental impact of industrial development. It passed the National Environment Quality Act in 1992 to set standards and guidelines for future development. These guidelines are designed to reduce air, water, and noise pollution. The traffic police periodically carry out campaigns to encourage automobile owners to use cleaner fuel alternatives. The Bangkok Metropolitan Authority is also promoting transportation via canals and rivers in the city to reduce road congestion.

POLLUTION FROM MINES

In 1992 villagers of Mae Moh, Lampang Province, reported headaches and respiratory problems such as breathing difficulties. These health problems were linked to air pollution from a power plant that ran on locally mined lignite, a form of coal with a high sulfur content. The plant's filters did little to reduce the dust in the plant's emissions, and the plant ran at full capacity even when the filters broke down. The adverse effects of this plant alarmed the people of Prachuap Khiri Khan, near Bangkok, where two lignite-powered plants were to be built in 1995. Residents opposed the project fiercely through demonstrations, forcing the government to stop the construction of the plants.

More recently, in 2003, lead mining has been linked to contamination of water sources in Thung Yai Naresuan Wildlife Sanctuary in Kanchanaburi Province, and zinc mines on the Thai-Burmese border are thought to have polluted waters in Mae Sot.

WATER POLLUTION

In the early 21st century, despite the protests of environmental groups, the Thai government started granting mining concessions in national parks. Developers argued that they could safely exploit underground resources. But history proves otherwise. Two decades ago, toxic waste from a lead mine in the Kanchanaburi forest reserve near the Myanmar border leaked into the Klity River. This river was an important source of water for the Karen peoples living along the Lower Klity. All of them now suffer from lead poisoning and face the risk of serious effects such as brain damage.

On December 26, 2004, following an undersea earthquake off the west coast of Sumatra, Indonesia, a massive tsunami was unleashed across the Indian Ocean that killed an estimated 230,000 people in 14 countries. Waves of up to 49 feet (15 m) high devastated coastal communities in Indonesia, Thailand, India, and Sri Lanka and were felt as far away as East Africa. With a magnitude of between 9.1 and 9.3, it was the third-largest earthquake recorded on a seismograph (an instrument used to measure movement in the earth). This megathrust earthquake caused the entire planet to vibrate as much as 0.4 of an inch (1 cm) and triggered smaller earthquakes as far away as Alaska.

The tsunami was the worst natural disaster ever to strike Thailand. The impact was felt almost two hours after the original earthquake, as the gigantic waves moved slowly through the shallow Andaman Sea off Thailand's west coast. Coastal towns and tourist resorts—especially the resort of Khao Lak and beaches on the island of Phuket—were particularly badly affected. It is estimated that more than 8,000 people died from the massive waves hitting low-lying beaches along Thailand's western coast. Few people recognized the telltale signs of an imminent tsunami, as the ocean *initially receded and frothed before huge waves swamped the coastline. Many Western tourists were vacationing in Thailand at the time, and recorded numerous, graphic reports and images of the damage sustained.*

The Thai government responded quickly to the disaster, providing medical assistance and humanitarian relief, with the army helping in the rescue operations, recovery, and cleanup. With the tsunami happening during the peak Christmas holiday season, the tourist industry was badly affected, as more than 4,000 foreigners from 37 countries were killed or injured in the disaster. Up to 120,000 people are thought to have had their livelihoods seriously affected, mainly in fishing- and tourist-related businesses. The government spent millions of dollars on the reconstruction of homes and roads and has been praised for its effective response to the disaster by the United Nations. The Thai government also established a National Disaster Warning Center and helped local businesses recover by offering credit, encouraging cooperatives, and developing alternative sources of income.

INTERNET LINKS

http://maps.grida.no/go/graphic/disappearing-forests

This website features a map that demonstrates the comparative extent of deforestation across mainland Southeast Asia between 1970 and 1990.

http://rainforest.mongabay.com/20thailand.htm

This website offers description and data on the state of Thailand's environment, with brief analysis of the main issues.

www.visit-chiang-mai-online.com/tsunami-thailand.html

This website provides an account with still photographs and videos of the 2004 tsunami swamping various locations in Thailand.

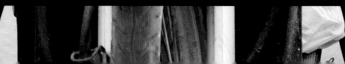

THAI

A Thai family on a scooter. The exact origins of the Thai people are debatable but they are believed to have first come from China.

6

M OST PEOPLE IN THAILAND CALL
themselves Thai, but the Thai are
only one of the related groups that
fall under the generic term Tai (or Dai, as it
is spelled in China).

THE TAI

Tai origins are hard to pinpoint. Some historians believe the Tai came
from northern Sichuan in southwestern China; others claim the Tai's first
home was in southeastern China, north of Vietnam. About 2,000 years
ago, the first Tai emigrants began moving south toward the provinces
of Yunnan and Guizhou. This migration was probably prompted by the
search for fertile land or to escape from oppressive overlords. By
the seventh or eighth century, some Tai had gone farther south into
Southeast Asia.

By the 13th century there were clearly defined branches of the
Tai in six countries. Today the Black Thai and the White Thai live in
Vietnam; the Lao Tai, the Phu Tai, and the Tai Phuan, in Laos. The Tai
Yuan, also known as Khon Muang, dominate the north of Thailand,
and the Siamese Thai populate the rest of Thailand. Most Tai Yai
(or Shan) live in Myanmar; the Ahom, a Thai Buddhist group, live in
northeastern India. In China, the Tai Lü dominate Xishuangbanna;
the Tai Ya and the Tai La inhabit the Red River area of Yunnan;
and the Tai Neua populate southwestern Yunnan.

The Thai people
are the main
ethnic group of
Thailand and are
part of the larger
Tai peoples
found in Thailand
and other parts
of Southeast
Asia including
southern China.
Their language
is the Thai
language, and
the majority
are Buddhists.

DEMOGRAPHY

Before any of the Tai migrated from China, Thailand was first settled by Negrito peoples from the south. They spread north into the heart of present-day Thailand, only to be forced to retreat later by the powerful Mon and Khmer.

A small number of these early migrants—called the Sakai, the Semang, or the Ngo—survive in four groups in the southernmost provinces where they reside in the jungles, hunting with blowpipes.

The ethnic makeup of Thailand's people has been mixed by war and long periods of living together. During the Ayutthaya period Burma, Chiang Mai, Luang Prabang, and Cambodia, the victors of major wars with Siam, took hundreds of thousands of prisoners back to their own countries.

The Mon—after being conquered by the Khmer, the Thai, and the Burmese—integrated well into the different cultures. They are hardly a distinct people any longer in Thailand, although they still have a strong community in Myanmar. This mixing among peoples helps account for the great ethnic diversity in Thailand.

With the end of the Burmese wars, Thailand became the destination of the hill peoples of neighboring countries. First it was the Karen from the west. Then, at the beginning of the 20th century, groups from Laos, Myanmar, Yunnan, and Guizhou started arriving. Most of them have settled in the north, where the terrain of hills and forests resembles the lands they left behind.

SINO-THAI AND THAI MUSLIMS

The Chinese—just over 14 percent of the population—make up the largest minority group in Thailand. They came from southern China, and most of them arrived in Thailand between 1860 and 1940. Of all the migrant Chinese in Southeast Asia, those in Thailand have integrated into the foreign society of their host country most successfully.

When the Chinese came to work or set up businesses, they had to learn Thai rather than colonial tongues. They became Buddhists but did not

One interesting group living in Nan Province, bordering Laos, is the Mlabri, whom Thai call the Phi Tong Luang, or "Spirits of the Yellow Leaves." They are a very small nomadic group who hunt and gather wild plants for food. Their name refers to their habit of migrating whenever the banana leaves, with which they make the roofs of their houses, turn yellow.

abandon their ancestral worship and customs. Today's Chinese, whether Thai or Sino-Thai, observe Buddhist rites and respect the importance of kinship groups, but they speak Thai and follow most Thai customs. After World War II, the Sino-Thai were further integrated into mainstream society, which prompted them to keep their money in Thailand rather than send it back to China.

Thai Muslims, whether the ethnic Thai or the Malays in the south, have not been so well assimilated. They make up 4.6 percent of the population. Most are Sunni Muslims living in fishing communities, which keeps them out of mainstream Thai society. Their children usually attend Islamic schools, for conservative parents object to the dress code and customs of the other schools. Although they may feel uncomfortable under a non-Muslim government, they have shown little support for separatist movements.

Muslim worshipers arriving at the mosque for their Friday prayers. The Muslim community is found mainly in southern Thailand.

PEOPLE OF ISAN

People of the northeast—Isan—call themselves Lao and speak a dialect closer to that of their relatives in Laos than that of the Thai. At the end of the 19th century this region split into dozens of small states run by local lords who paid tribute to the king of Siam. The northeast has suffered from its distance, both physical and political, from Bangkok. The Thai government has largely neglected the development of the region. Compared with the rest of Thailand, the northeast has few roads and schools, and incomes are low.

Most Lao are rice farmers, and many of the farmers are tenant farmers. The Lao in northeastern Thailand form about a third of Thailand's population. In addition to the Lao, there are about 1 million Khmer and 400,000 Kui, a related group, residing in Isan. Most live near the Cambodian border.

TRADITIONAL DRESS

Traditional Thai clothing was not tailored to fit a person exactly. Instead it was made of narrow strips of woven silk or cotton that were joined, folded, or tucked to serve as various garments.

A woman in traditional Thai dress.

For women, the basic dress was a *pha sin* (pah sin), which consisted of two or three strips of cloth sewn into a tube that was worn around the waist and tucked in at the navel. Another narrow strip was wrapped around the chest. Men wore a strip of cloth tied between the legs and around the waist known as *pha khao ma* (pa kao mah). Both men and women carried their belongings in cloth bags slung over the shoulder.

Pha sin could be plain but were usually striped. People from one location or ethnic group often wore the same pattern on their *pha sin*. The lower cloths were often intricately embroidered.

In the 19th century, Thai monarchs encouraged the Thai to wear Western-style clothes, such as shirts for men. For both sexes, tailored clothes became fashionable. After World War II the government promoted a complete changeover to Western-style clothing. Now the *pha sin* is regarded by some as the dress of the poor or the traditional.

PEOPLE OF THE HILLS

Hill people in the north make their villages out of jungle materials, and some still practice the most ancient form of agriculture—the slash-and-burn method.

Every winter, farmers clear a patch of forest, then burn the felled trees and shrubs. The ashes fertilize the otherwise poor soil enough to grow rice and other crops for one or two years. The farmers then abandon that field and start all over again on a new one. They return to the original patch after a period of up to 10 years.

Many of the hill people came from neighboring countries. They left their original homeland because of wars and rebellions. In Myanmar and Laos, they did not have enough land to grow rice successfully. Therefore, they turned to growing opium—which can be grown on the same field for 10 years—as a cash crop to barter for rice. This became a huge problem for the Thai authorities when groups of opium farmers, fleeing ethnic unrest in Myanmar and Laos, began moving into secluded Thai forests. In some cases, the refugees continued the opium business in the forests.

The Thai government began taking action against this in 1976, and today most opium farmers have been persuaded to raise other crops instead. Still, increasing migration across the borders has put a strain on the area. This has prompted the government to begin reforestation projects, introduce stricter border rules to control migration, and even throw out or relocate whole groups of people.

A woman from the Akha hill tribe wearing a traditional silver headpiece.

SMALLER GROUPS

THE KAREN number around 400,000 and make up half of the hill population. They usually live along Thailand's western border. They make their homes in the hills, up to an elevation of 1,650 feet (503 m). The Karen also farm on the plains.

THE MEO, or Hmong, total 151,000. One of the largest southern Chinese ethnic groups, they entered Thailand via Laos and have spread to 13 provinces. The women wear skirts of batik cloth, and both sexes wear embroidered clothing.

THE YAO There are 40,000 Yao, or Mien. The Yao came from southeastern China and have retained many of their Chinese beliefs and customs. They can be considered the most "Chinese" of the Chinese groups in Thailand. They use Chinese characters for their songs and stories. The women wear fully embroidered pants and black turbans.

THE LAHU, or Musur, number 85,000. Originating in Yunnan, they are divided into six groups that wear different costumes. Many are converting to Christianity, although most still worship a variety of gods.

THE AKHA There are 55,000 Akha. Originally from Yunnan, then Myanmar, they live in areas up to 5,000 feet (1,524 m) above sea level. Their villages are distinguished by a pair of gates and a large swing, and the women wear heavy silver headdresses and beautiful jackets.

THE LISU total 30,000. Also from Yunnan, they reside on hillsides at elevations of 3,000 feet (914 m). Their culture displays Chinese influences. For example, they celebrate Chinese New Year and eat with chopsticks. Lisu women wear bright tunics with striped shoulders.

Smaller groups of hill peoples include the forest-dwelling Mlabri, who are the most primitive of all the hill groups, the Mon-Khmer people such as the Lawa, and in Nan Province, the Htin and the Khamu.

The Lisu people gathering together for New Year's celebrations.

REFUGEES

Thailand has been more than a nervous witness to wars plaguing its neighbors. From 1975 to 1980 political terror and economic turmoil prompted more than a million people to flee Laos, Vietnam, and Cambodia to UN-managed refugee camps along Thailand's eastern border.

The influx of refugees and continued fighting in Cambodia also temporarily displaced 250,000 Thai. Thousands more from Myanmar sought safe haven along the Thai western border, especially in 1996 and 1998 after major military campaigns in that country designed to crush ethnic minorities' resistance to the government. Fighting still occasionally spills into Thai territory, disrupts border trade, and exacerbates relations between the two countries.

INTERNET LINKS

http://countrystudies.us/thailand/48.htm

This website provides comprehensive information about the Chinese in Thailand. It also includes information about the historic role of the Chinese as middlemen and their contribution to the Thai economy and politics.

www.tayara.com/club/hilltribe.htm

This website provides in-depth information about the history of Thailand's fascinating hill tribes, including the Mien, the Lahu, the Lisu, the Akha, the Hmong, and the Karen.

www.thailandsworld.com/index.cfm?p=3

This website of Discover Asia introduces diverse peoples of Thailand, including ethnic and nonethnic Thai. It also provides information about various hill tribes. A short section on famous Thai personalities is included on the site.

LIFESTYLE

A bustling Chang Mai street

7

ESPITE THE PRESENCE OF cosmopolitan cultures, social and even professional life in Thailand is still characterized by a set of traditional behaviors.

Modernization may bring rapid changes to Thai society, with new social classes arising and old ones declining. But many of the principles of behavior and values remain the same. To understand the "Thai way," let's start with a few basic points.

Jai yen (jai yen), or "cool heart," is a key requirement in all social gatherings. It means the ability to accept most things with grace and calm. Its opposite, always considered a social wrong, is any showing of *jai rohn* (jai rohn), or "hot heart," of which anger, impatience, and visible displeasure are examples.

Krengjai (KREN-jai) is translated as "consideration," but it specifically means a demonstration of consideration for the feelings of others, particularly one's superiors. As such, *krengjai* contains the notions of humility, politeness, respect, and obedience. This principle is stressed throughout every Thai's upbringing and is important in all forms of Thai social behavior.

Rules of respect within the family are reflected in the language Thai use in social situations. A younger member in the family always refers to an older one as *phii* (pee). In turn, the older member calls the younger *nong* (nawng). In their interaction with the wider society, Thai still refer to older people as *phii* and younger people as *nong*. They follow this rule regardless of the status and identity of the people they are dealing with, be they members of the family, close friends, or strangers.

Present-day Thailand is both modern and traditional. Institutions and laws ensure that anyone with ambition and talent can rise in society. But Thai culture has old and deep roots, and society is established in customs and attitudes that are centuries old.

Thai believe they are born into a place in society that is determined by their karma, the cumulative effect of thoughts and deeds in their past lives. However, with acts of *tam boon* (tahm boon)—making merit—they can better their social position. Generous deeds such as feeding monks, giving alms, and praying frequently at the local *wat* (waht), or temple, count as acts of *tam boon*. Some Thai believe that the merit they get for their acts of *tam boon* can be transferred to another person, such as their parents.

THE THAI WAY

In dealing with people, the Thai always acknowledge the other person's higher or lower status. Restraint and courtesy are the focal points of Thai social relations. Both speech and gestures feature these qualities. The type of greeting the Thai use depends on the rank of the person addressed. Thai people respect patrons, employers, teachers, older people, royalty, and monks, whom even kings treat respectfully. People who belong to the same age group and status may refer to one another as *khun* (koon), which means "your goodness." As these people become friends, they often stop referring to each other by that title.

Much communication is expressed through body language. In general, there is a set of social and conventional gestures the Thai use to make themselves understood. The most complex gestures are reserved for the royal family or Buddhist monks. A general rule of gesture that most Thai people observe is lowering one's head and bowing slightly when walking past someone of higher rank. They also frown on pointing at things with the foot, which is considered a low-ranking body part.

Being blunt or outspoken is generally discouraged in Thailand. It is viewed as a socially bad trait, a threat to harmony. The Thai use of pronouns reflects

The *wai* (weye) is the ancient Thai tradition of saying hello or good-bye. It is made by raising both hands, palms joined, to lightly touch the body between the chest and forehead, something like the praying action. The higher the hands are raised, the greater the respect given. The junior person always gives the *wai* before the senior; for an older person to *wai* the younger first is considered bad luck. The *wai* may be done standing, sitting, walking, or even on the sickbed.

this. The Thai language book used at Bangkok's American University Alumni Language Center lists 11 words for *you*. But in ordinary conversation, Thai people usually avoid *you* and use the individual's name instead. Nor do they use the word *I*, unless absolutely necessary.

The extraordinary attention given to keeping social harmony comes from a village-based culture. The economy of a village often requires all villagers to cooperate and help in such matters as rice planting and harvesting and flood control and relief. Individual concerns tend to come second to the interests of the community. Harmony governs life. Religious beliefs also support this. *Jai rohn* actions are considered by most Thai people to be a challenge to household spirits, who would then punish the guilty party for the disturbance.

The Thai way also provides guidelines for handling conflicts and criticism. Both *jai yen* and *krengjai* come into play here. A Thai will never criticize a superior publically—not just because of the loss of face but also because it would challenge the superior's right to be obeyed. Criticism and changes are made behind the scenes.

THE SMILE

Thai codes of behavior, based on restraint and courtesy, often discourage a hearty belly laugh, but Thai do smile a lot. Amusement and expressing thanks are two obvious reasons to smile.

Thai people also tend to smile in order to sidestep difficult questions, to excuse any lack of courtesy, and to cover their embarrassment. However, the readiness with which a Thai smiles is one of the more charming aspects of the Thai way.

FAMILY

In Thai society the immediate family is much more important than the extended family. In addition, the mother's side of the family ranks higher than the father's, especially in the north and the northeast. Thai do not form kinship groups as do people in Chinese and Indian societies.

Thai give their newborn babies cloths with the drawing of a giant to protect them from evil spirits. This giant, Taowetsuwan, is much feared by spirits and is a famous personality in Thai myths. Legend says that Taowetsuwan was offering food to monks one day and spilled some hot liquid on a monk's foot. As the monk yelped in pain, Taowetsuwan laughed. For this, he was sent to the world of the giants. Even though he became king of the giants, he suffered much because his feet constantly felt as if hot liquid were being poured on them.

Members of the immediate family are often very close to one another. Relationships are based on the younger generation honoring and obeying the older generation and being humble before them. Younger siblings obey older brothers and sisters, whereas the older ones assume responsibility for the behavior of the younger ones.

Thai women play vital roles within the family and the community, for they nurture their children and provide food for the community's monks when the monks make their morning rounds.

A family of four ride together on a scooter. Families in Thailand are usually close-knit.

There are Thai men who keep alive the tradition of having a *mia noi* (mee-AH noi), or "minor wife." However, they try to keep their mistresses secret, as it is not a socially acceptable practice.

BIRTH

For the educated Thai, there are scores of magazines and books to consult for the latest medical information. In the rural areas, however, many still believe it is the spirits known as *phi* (pee) who allow children to be born. They believe that within three days of birth, the *phi* will come to view the baby and, if they like him or her, will take the infant away.

Believers try to please these spirits with tiny food offerings on a platter made from banana leaves or sheaths made from the stem of a plantain (a relative of the banana), hoping that this will make the spirits leave the baby alone. Meanwhile, it is believed that no one should compliment the mother on the baby's fine appearance or else the spirits will overhear and become more determined to snatch the child. If the appropriate steps are taken and all goes well, after the fourth day the child belongs to its parents.

But for the first month, a child is not considered a family member, a custom perhaps dating back to earlier times when infants frequently died before they were a month old. After the first month, the child becomes the happy family's son or daughter.

In some cases Thai parents do not name their child until he or she is one month old. Parents may then give the child a long Sanskrit name, which the child might not learn until he or she reaches adulthood. Parents often name their girls after flowers and precious gems, whereas boys receive names referring to victory, courage, or wisdom.

Since Thai first names are usually long, often having three or four syllables, most Thai also have a nickname given by their parents. Thai are called by their nicknames in the family and among friends and colleagues. The nickname may be the name of an animal such as "bird," a fruit such as "apple," a color, or even an English name such as "Tim."

A Karen hill tribe woman with her child.

GROWING UP

Most children start elementary school at the age of six or seven. At that age, their parents expect them to be more self-sufficient and to take on small responsibilities. Still, a bit of pampering continues, and it is common to see adults giving up their seats to schoolchildren on the bus.

In the past, Thai boys kept a knot of hair on top of their heads; many believed that this warded off illness. At the age of 11 or 13—never an even number—they would get all their hair cut off in a public ceremony in January.

All Thai children attend six years of elementary school free of charge. Consequently Thailand has one of the most literate populations in the world. In the first three years of elementary school, children are taught basic Thai, introductory math and science, music, and drawing. In their fourth year they begin studying Thai history. The following year will see them studying world history, geography, religion, and literature. After elementary school comes six years of high school, but this is neither compulsory nor free. Technical and

Most rural folk marry between New Year's Day and the planting of the annual rice crop in late spring or early summer. Most Thai marriages take place in even-numbered lunar months. Thai believe that since weddings involve two people, wedding months should be multiples of two. The best lunar months are the second, fourth, sixth, and eighth. However, the ninth month is also preferred, simply because the number nine is associated with progress and wealth in Thailand.

vocational schools are alternatives to academic high schools. For those who do go beyond elementary school, military training begins in the ninth grade. Drills dominate the first two years, after which boys are taught the use of firearms.

MARRIAGE

Young Thai men and women, except royalty and conservative Muslims, choose life partners for themselves. Although they would prefer to obtain their parents' approval, they may marry without it. There are many opportunities for Thai youth to meet the opposite sex, since young women are allowed to socialize in mixed company.

Traditional Thai attitudes to marriage are changing. Most people now marry at a later age than did their parents and grandparents. Many young women are postponing marriage to develop their careers. It is no longer unusual to meet women who are over 30 years old and unmarried. But in remote rural areas couples are still marrying young, some before they reach the age of 19.

Traditional Thai marriages are usually performed by as many as nine Buddhist monks. The ceremony begins in the morning with the happy couple wearing headdresses joined by a length of white string. Monks place a white cord called a *sai sin* (seye seen) around the ground where the couple stand, marking it off as a sacred zone. A half-hour of chanting and blessing follows, and the senior monk sprinkles holy water over the couple, using a sprig of Chinese gooseberry.

In the evening purified water is poured over the joined hands of the bride and the groom. After a rousing wedding party, the next event is a trip to the bride's house. In former times the groom was required to build a house for himself and his bride in his father-in-law's compound. Nowadays he merely presents gifts to the bride's family. Generally the party has to pass through "toll gates" erected by the children at the bride's house. It is common practice for the children to ask for a "toll."

Among the hill people and in upcountry villages, there are often strict rules regarding marriage. Members of hill groups do not marry within the same clan. Among the Akha, there must be seven generations without a common ancestor. Among the Meo, couples must be roughly the same age or at least less than a generation apart.

In minority groups marriage negotiations revolve around such things as a proper "bride price" (among the Yao), terms of gifts and services (among the Lisu), or how long the groom will live with the bride's family (a Karen custom). The actual ceremony finds the couple dressed in grand clothing and the bride playing the role of the shy maiden. The dress of an unmarried woman differs from that of a married one, so single men know whom to court! Funerals and weddings, which usually draw a crowd, are ideal opportunities to meet potential partners.

CAREER

For young Thai people with ambition, 12 years of school are not enough. They will try to gain admission to one of the 16 state and numerous private colleges and universities.

A couple having water poured over their hands during their traditional wedding ceremony.

Among the oldest and most famous of these universities are Chulalongkorn and Thammasat. Both are situated in Bangkok. The latter was founded in 1934 after the constitutional monarchy was formed. Entrance to both of these universities is very difficult, whereas admission to some of the other universities is less competitive. In some of these universities class attendance is voluntary.

The government recruits its officers from among the graduates of Chulalongkorn and Thammasat, as do top corporations, usually after the student has gone abroad to acquire a master's degree.

Thai companies set very high standards for their employees. Not only do prospective employees have to be well educated, but they also have to be respected in Thai society. The civil service wants graduates from "a socially acceptable family," whereas newspaper advertisements for managerial candidates state that applicants must have "good social connections."

Besides government service and business, other professions rated highly by Thai society include bankers and stockbrokers, engineers and technical specialists, doctors, judges, monks, hotel managers, pilots, and—especially among rural folk—military and police officers.

FREE TIME

Many Thai like to spend their free time with other people, even going on vacations in groups, to places such as natural and historical sites.

Thai like to eat out, not because they dislike cooking but because they enjoy the social scene. Office workers and student groups often organize picnics or weekend seaside trips, and the zest for joining the crowd peaks at weddings, funerals, and other ceremonies.

Urbanites have all the usual distractions available in the cities— television, movie theaters, bars, discos, nightclubs, concerts, shopping malls, night markets, and so forth. Those in the countryside do not have such options, although movie theaters, televisions, and DVDs seem to be everywhere. Moreover, there are more than 500 local radio stations in the country, with some broadcasting in dialects of the minority peoples. In remote areas and hill villages the main activity is visiting friends and relatives. A courting ground is a unique feature in Akha villages; it provides a place where young singles meet, sing, dance, and amuse themselves.

DEATH

When ill, the Thai can choose from among several types of remedies. Besides the variety of drugs and treatments available in the markets, they may try either Thai or Chinese traditional herbal medicine.

Thai Buddhists believe in an afterlife and reincarnation. When a person dies at home, the corpse is kept three to seven days before it is removed.

If death occurs elsewhere, the body of the deceased is taken to a temple and cremated. This usually occurs within a week.

Buddhists believe that a lavish funeral can improve the person's next life. Consequently funerals are usually as grand as the wealth of a family will permit, involving many gifts, feasting, and even a film or theater presentation.

On the first day of the wake, it is customary that the family of the deceased bathes, perfumes, and dresses the corpse before laying it out on a mat. They place a one-baht coin in the mouth, fold the hands

Plaques of the deceased on temple grounds at Don Muang in Bangkok.`

into a *wai,* and tie the wrists, neck, and ankles with white thread. The coin is a reminder to the living that people leave all their worldly possessions behind when they die. The white thread symbolizes the ties that the deceased established in life: The loop around the neck symbolizes attachment to the deceased's offspring; the bound wrists, the attachment to marriage; and the bound ankles, attachment to property.

The mourners insert into the palms of the deceased a banknote, two flowers, and two candles. Then they seal the mouth and eyes with wax and put the body into a coffin with the head facing west, the direction of the setting sun.

Next to the head of the coffin the family lights a lamp on the ground, where they put a sleeping mat, a blanket, plates, food, clothing, and a knife for use in the afterlife. Guests donate banknotes, which are fixed onto bamboo sticks and planted like flags in the side of the coffin. Monks chant for three days beside the corpse, eating their meals in the home of the deceased. At the end of the wake, the coffin is carried feet first out of the house. If there is a ladder leading to the house, the ladder is reversed. Water jars placed at the entrance are turned upside down. Thai believe that this will discourage the soul from trying to reenter the home.

On the way to the cremation site, mourners scatter rice grains to soothe the deceased's spirit. Funerals can be grand; whole villages sometimes participate in the event. Buffalo are slaughtered, and the meat is divided among the clan of the deceased or the village. Memorial services are held after three months and again on the one-year anniversary of the death.

THAI HOUSES

The traditional Thai house is a rectangular building made of strong hardwoods such as teakwood and stands on poles, with the living quarters raised above the ground. Since as much as half of the year is wet or damp, this is an altogether healthy living arrangement. The space beneath the living quarters is left open, and in dry weather it serves as a place where activities such as weaving are carried out. The upper level generally includes an L-shape terrace and a sheltered veranda. The living area is generally divided into a dining room, which is also a room to receive guests, and the sleeping quarters.

A traditional Thai spirit house. It is common to see these in the compounds of houses and on the grounds of apartments in Thailand.

Upon entry to the house, shoes are removed and left at the stairs on the ground floor, where there may also be a water jar and dipper for a person to clean up before going to the upper floor. The upper floor is often swept and washed down.

The house itself sits in a compound along with smaller buildings. The compound is usually surrounded by a wall. The area that houses the grain and rice-pounding shed is separate from the house, while the kitchen and water-storage room are attached to the main building. In Bangkok, many of these teak houses can be found on the shores on the Chayo Praya River. The most famous one in Bangkok is Jim Thompson's house near Siam Square.

Thai in the Central Plains draw their water from rivers and *khlong*, whereas those in the north and the northeast rely on artesian wells (boreholes from which groundwater spouts due to pressure in the ground).

In urban towns and cities including Bangkok, many people live in large condominiums or high-rise apartments. These buildings often include leisure facilities such as swimming pools and tennis courts as well as services such as a laundry, a mini supermarket, a café, and a beauty salon. Others live in modern houses built with cement and brick. The wealthy in Thailand live in luxurious homes, which are similar to those in Western countries. Some of these are opulent and palatial suburban estate houses, which many Thai aspire to live in.

An important additional building that completes the Thai home is the spirit house. This resembles a miniature temple and is mounted on a stand. Small offerings are regularly left around the spirit house for the guardian spirit of the compound. The offerings usually include flowers, food, and incense. This is a custom that illustrates Thailand's pre-Buddhist roots.

In the countryside, farmers' houses are usually made of palm thatch, sticks, and straw tightly stacked around tall, stout poles.

INTERNET LINKS

http://cultureandreligionofthailand.blogspot.com/2007/09/thai-funeral.html

This website provides a collection of articles on many aspects of cultural and religious life in Thailand, including marriage ceremonies, funeral rites, social hierarchy, and the position of women in Thai society.

www.moe.go.th/English/

The official website of Thailand's Ministry of Education links to education news, education statistics, and relevant articles on education in the country.

www.nationmaster.com/country/th-thailand/lif-lifestyle

This website provides comprehensive coverage of interesting Thai lifestyle facts and figures, including the number of roller coasters and amateur radio operators.

RELIGION

Wat Phra Sing. The predominant religion in Thailand is Buddhism. Buddhist temples can be found all over the country.

8

ALMOST 95 PERCENT OF THE THAI population are Buddhists. Muslims, making up 4.6 percent of the total population, are the second-largest religious group. The other groups include Christians and Hindus. The hill groups practice ancestor worship.

Buddhism, the state, and the monarchy are the three official "pillars" of the nation. The king is considered the protector of all religions. Since the early 17th century, when Ayutthaya kings permitted Christian missionaries to build the first churches, the Thai people have enjoyed religious freedom.

Devotees offering incense and prayers at the Wat Suthat in Bangkok.

Monks have a high-profile status in Thai society and can be seen everywhere on the streets, in temples, and in other public places. They depend totally on the community for support, making the rounds with their bowls early each morning, asking for alms.

Before Buddhism sank its roots into Thai society, Thai settlers were practicing the sophisticated religion of the Mon and the Khmer. Through them, Thai had adopted the Hindu view of kingship, the caste system of the Brahmins, and the worship of Erawan, the Elephant God. Hindu influence can also be seen in classical literature, such as the story of Rama and Sita in the *Ramakien*, the Thai version of the *Ramayana*.

Early Thai practiced animism, or the worship of natural objects. Their beliefs continue to influence present-day Thai, especially minority groups, who believe that the world is filled with *phi*—spirits of dead people, animals, and trees—that must be pleased lest they upset life's harmony and bring poor harvests. There are various ways of dealing with *phi*. For example, the Thai build miniature houses on altars of food and flowers in front of trees believed to be inhabited by *phi*. Acts of merit at temples also help in fighting evil *phi*.

BUDDHISM

The Hindu god, Ganesh, also known as the Elephant God, in a temple in Chang Mai.

Buddhism became the state religion during the Sukhothai period. The form of Buddhism practiced in Thailand is called Theravada, which translates as "the teaching of the elders." Theravada Buddhism was introduced by monks from Sri Lanka who traveled through Thailand, Myanmar, Laos, and Cambodia. It flourished under King Ramkhamhaeng's grandson, King Lithai (reigned 1347—68), who summarized more than 30 volumes of Buddhist scripture into one book, the *Tribhumikatha*. Some pre-Buddhist beliefs were absorbed into Buddhism. For example, Thai Buddhists still believe in *khwan* (kwahn), or spirits that reside in lifeless objects and parts of the body.

Groups of Theravada Buddhist monks, called the Sangha, live in temple compounds, where they produce Thai handicrafts. An alms bowl, a daily meal, one set of robes, shelter for meditation and rest, and medication in times of illness are all the Sangha require to live. The Sangha are supported by donations from Buddhists who believe such acts will decrease their suffering in this life and the next.

Between the 13th and 15th centuries, the Sangha became the central religious institution in Thai society. Under King Chulalongkorn, a standard system of education for monks was established, and in 1902 the Sangha were united under one leadership.

BUDDHIST PRACTICES

Buddhists believe that suffering exists because of human desire and attachment; to eliminate these weaknesses, they observe the Eightfold Path. The strictest followers of the Eightfold Path are the monks.

Most monks in a monastery are novices, but some have chosen to make a career out of monkhood. Monks are highly respected in Thai society. Thus,

Monks at morning prayer at Wat Pho.

In Thailand, animism and Buddhism are combined in many ways. For instance, children from Buddhist families often wear charms on their arms or legs to ward off evil spirits. Thai Buddhists do not seem to care whether the charm is a Buddhist amulet or one prepared by the village witch doctor. They care mainly about one thing—not to "offend the spirits."

SUMMER AT THE *WAT*

Some years before the fall of Sukhothai, King Lithai temporarily left his throne to spend some time as a monk. He thereby started a custom that has been followed by Thai men ever since. Every male is expected to spend a few months in a monastery, and the most popular time for this is during the last three months of the rainy season. This period coincides with the Buddhist Lent, which begins in the middle of July.

Thai believe there are several benefits to this. If a boy becomes a novice monk, his mother will not enter hell; if he becomes a full monk, his father will also not enter hell. Government servants who elect to spend a summer in a wat *receive full pay during their stay. But the real benefit lies in the study of Buddhist teachings. A stint in a monastery is expected to remind Thai men of the laws of Buddhism.*

Thai men can assure themselves of social advancement if they get through the various levels of religious schools. For a rural youth from an average background, the monastery is one way to a better life, and if he is not committed to his religious position, he can leave the monkhood anytime.

Monks follow a tough code of regulations. They chant mornings and evenings, listen to scripture readings, study the ancient texts, and then retire for the day. Each day starts at around 5 A.M.

Lay Thai people sometimes ask monks for blessings. For example, monks may be asked to bless buildings under construction or the souls of recently deceased relatives or friends.

Thai Buddhists make trips to the temple whenever they feel the need to and on religious holidays. Their offerings are usually jasmine flowers and incense sticks. Sometimes they dab some gold leaf onto statues of the Buddha. Fish or birds are often sold near Thai temples. Buddhists buy them to release as acts of merit. Occasionally a Buddhist may hire a troupe of temple dancers, either to ask for a favor or to give thanks to a god.

OTHER RELIGIONS

Many of Thailand's Chinese minority practice Taoism. Chinese temples display ancestral tablets on decorated altars and shrines dedicated to legendary Chinese heroes or heroines. Some Chinese practice Mahayana Buddhism, which reached Thailand in the ninth century.

Chinese events can become occasions for acts of self-mutilation and walking on hot coals. One such example is the Phuket Vegetarian Festival, which starts the Taoist Lent in October.

The Church of Santa Cruz, located along the Chao Phraya River.

Christian missionaries helped educate King Mongkut, who opened the country to the West. The missionaries also started Thailand's first printing press in 1835 and introduced schools and modern medical practices.

Thailand's Muslims live in the southern provinces. There are about 3,500 mosques in Thailand and several hundred Islamic schools in cities and villages throughout Thailand. The city of Pattani alone has more than 500 mosques. Most Muslims attend religious or Islamic schools, and Muslim children who attend Thai schools attend weekly Islamic religious instruction.

Hill people usually practice their own religions, which are closely connected to their agricultural lifestyle. For example, Karen hold ritual feasts and celebrations to honor the territorial guardian spirit, known as the Lord of Water and Land. They do this twice a year, before planting and before harvesting. The hill groups believe that these rites will bring good harvests. Some minority groups, such as the Meo and the Yao, follow several Chinese or Taoist customs.

Christianity has influenced up to a third of the minority peoples, many of whom are refugees. This is partly because of the work of Thai Christians and foreign missionaries. The small but rapidly growing Christian community resides mainly in the north.

A palmist working with a client in his shop.

FORTUNE-TELLING

Fortune-telling has always been especially popular in Thailand but became more so after the 1997 financial crisis, when people sought reassurance about their future. The most commonly seen fortune-tellers use a deck of 32 cards. They assign one card to the client, then lay the rest of the cards around it and interpret the arrangement.

Palmistry is also common. If a palmist has the client's astrological birth information (especially the time), he or she claims to be able to predict the future by reading the lines on the palms. Experts say there are major lines that represent the head, the heart, life, fate, success, and so forth and that

THE GENEROUS PRINCE

Of all the stories in Thai religious literature, the most popular one is that of Prince Vessandorn, an incarnation of the Buddha.

In the story, Vessandorn gives away the country's prized white elephant to foreigners because he believes this will help the foreigners relieve their land of drought. But because of this, his own people demand his exile. So he departs, giving away his possessions, even his children. The god Indra at one point tricks Vessandorn into giving his wife to him, but later he returns her to the prince. After some complications, Vessandorn is recalled by his father and reunited with his children.

The tale portrays Vessandorn as a role model of generosity and religious merit. It is recited every year at the wat *on the full-moon night at the end of the Buddhist Lent.*

the patterns can reveal both the present and the future. Sometimes palmists even take a palm print to better check all the tiny branch lines.

THAI ASTROLOGY

In Siam it was the astrologer's duty to fix the time for a military battle or attack to begin. Astrology is still taken seriously for ceremonies in Thailand. Events ranging from state rituals to the laying of foundation stones of buildings must always begin at a precise time, which astrologers determine. They read horoscopes to determine the suitability of prospective marriage partners or to advise for or against business investments.

MIND-BODY THERAPY

Thai massage, thought to have developed in the second or third century B.C., is a combination of local folk medicine and Chinese acupuncture. Thai massage involves pressure on invisible energy lines running throughout the body. The masseuse presses or inserts needles at several points of the body to help distribute the patient's "energy flow" more evenly. This is said to relieve stress, improve general health, and increase one's life span.

Two hundred years ago, King Rama III ordered monks at Wat Po to carve the instructions and principles of Thai massage on slabs of stone. These stone slabs are still at Wat Po. The monastery is currently one of the most popular places for Thai people to learn the art of traditional massage.

AMULETS

Almost all Thai men and many women wear or carry amulets of some sort. Some wear as many as 10 at a time to protect themselves from harm ranging from accidents to gunfire to snakebites.

Makers of amulets have adopted religious symbols in their designs. Many Thai wear amulets of the Buddha and other religious images. Buddhist mantras written in the Khmer language are stuffed into tiny cylinders and worn around the neck. Other amulets include stones and seeds, tiger teeth, and boar tusks. Sometimes the amulets represent figures of royalty. For example, the King Chulalongkorn amulet was especially popular during the reign of the king. The king's portrait also appeared on a range of objects, from coffeepots to statues.

Magic charms may be purchased from stands set up near popular temples or on busy market streets. Some, such as special mantras, must be obtained from "spirit doctors" or "trance mediums" who can recommend the type of talisman required. There are even regular publications of stories about amulets and articles with expert advice on how to tell a real amulet from a false one. There are also stories of wearers who have survived horrible experiences because of their charms.

The most permanent sort of amulet is the mantra tattooed onto the body—usually on the chest or the arms—and always done in Khmer lettering. Rituals accompany the work, intended either to promote healing or to prevent harm from spirits. This sort of tattooing is popular in the north and the northeast, among both Thai and hill groups. In some cases the tattoos are done by Buddhist monks. The monks use a sharpened steel instrument 2 feet (61 cm) long and shaped like a rod. While they tattoo, they chant prayers. Some common patterns found in Thai tattoos include the tiger and the lizard, which represent prosperity and good luck. When the tattoos are completed, the monks bless them.

A different kind of body decoration existed in the past among men in the northern regions. They underwent an operation for several days that left them completely tattooed from the waist to the kneecaps. It was considered a test of their ability to withstand the pain. This custom was adopted from the ethnic practices of the Shan.

In 1770 the Burmese king ordered all Thai males in Burmese territory to be tattooed. The order never reached most of the country, and so neither did the custom. It appears, however, that men in northern Thailand did follow the order. The temple murals of the north show men in loincloths with bold, dark-blue tattoos on their thighs.

INTERNET LINKS

www.seasite.niu.edu:85/Thai/Islam_in_Thailand/contents.htm

This is the official website of the Center for Southeast Asian Studies of Northern Illinois University. This site provides comprehensive information about Islam in Thailand, including an overview, media coverage, selected readings, and images.

www.thaibuddhist.com/

This website is dedicated to understanding Buddhism as practiced in Thailand. This site incorporates links to Buddha images, Buddhist temples, Buddhist festivals, and articles about "making merit" and life as a novice monk.

www.thailandlife.com/thai-buddhist/index.php

This site provides a brief account of Thai Buddhist practices and beliefs as well as links to many other aspects of Thai Buddhism, including Wisakha Puja Day, the story of Mahajanaka, and the life of the Buddha.

LANGUAGE

เรามุ่งมั่นในการดำเนินธุรกิจ
เกื้อหนุนประโยชน์สูงสุดต่อ

A Thai schoolboy reads a book while waiting for his bus at a bus stop.

9

THE NATIONAL LANGUAGE OF Thailand, taught in all schools, is known as standard or central Thai and also Siamese or Bangkok Thai. It is the main Thai dialect spoken in the Central Plains.

Altogether, standard Thai and Thai dialects are the mother tongues of more than 80 percent of the population. The Teochew dialect of Chinese is the language of about 10 percent of the population.

Mon-Khmer speakers make up 3 percent of the population. The majority of these speakers are Cambodians, followed by Kui, Mon, Lawa, Htin, and Khamu. Malays in the south speak the Yawi dialect of the Malay language and account for about another 3 percent of the population.

Although nearly everyone in the country has at least some knowledge of the standard Thai dialect, many Thai-even ethnic Thai-speak one of a variety of dialects.

A newspaper and magazine stall vendor.

The Meo and Yao languages are related to the Austro-Thai language family, which probably expanded from Taiwan southward to the islands of Southeast Asia. The Yao use the older, more complex form of Chinese written characters, known as *fan ti zi* (fun tee tze), rather than the simplified version, or *jian ti zi* (chyen tee tze).

Karen dialects, such as the monosyllabic tongues spoken by more than a billion people in Central and Southeast Asia, are Sino-Tibetan in origin. The Tibeto-Burman languages, of the Sino-Tibetan family, are spoken by the Akha, the Lahu, and the Lisu.

THAI AND ITS DIALECTS

Thai words are monosyllabic and have five tones: mid, low, falling, high, and rising. Thai words are concepts in themselves and do not change according to case, number, or gender. The same word may be a noun, a verb, or an adjective depending on where it stands in the sentence. The basic sentence structure is subject-verb-object. Modifiers follow their relevant words. Articles, prepositions, and conjunctions are rare.

During the Ayutthayan period from the 1300s to the 1700s, the Thai incorporated many words from the Indian languages of Sanskrit and Pali into their language. These words, such as *rat* (raht), meaning "state," and *theep* (teep), meaning "God," were used in governmental matters and religious affairs. But the pronunciation was altered to make them sound like Thai words. Inflections and accents were also dropped. The Mon and the Khmer also borrowed heavily from Pali and Sanskrit. This is why everyday Siamese Thai and Khmer share one-third of their words.

Among the features adopted from the Khmer language was the use of prefixes and infixes, which are linguistic elements added at the beginning of or inserted into the word to modify the meaning and to change grammatical tense. With so many monosyllabic words, the language is filled with words that sound alike. For those with identical tones that need to be clarified, people either add words that clarify their meaning or substitute words of the same meaning.

In the Thai language two important words people use to express politeness are *krap* (krahp), used by men, and *ka* (kah), used by women. They are used after every request and reply.

Thai dialects exhibit similar grammar and structure. The main differences are in vocabulary. Each of Thailand's four main regions—the north, the northeast, the central, and the south—has its own dialect. Pak Tai, the language of the south, is close to Siamese or Central Thai but has a strong tendency toward shortened words and fast speech. The less educated people in the regions far from Bangkok may not understand all the Central Thai they hear, but because of its tremendous media exposure—radio, television, and movies reach everywhere—they can decipher most of it.

Thai language has also taken words from English. Numerous English-language newspapers and magazines serve Thailand, and provincial newspapers are published once every 10 days with the results of the national lottery. Of these, the *Bangkok Post* has the best international news, whereas *The Nation* is known for its features and opinions. Words of Malay-Javanese origin have also found their way into Thai speech, thanks to the popularity of Javanese tales since the beginning of the reign of the Chakri kings.

A *tuk-tuk* (motorized rickshaw) driver reading the papers during a break.

Some Thai proverbs are quite similar to those used in the English language. For example, "escape from a tiger and meet a crocodile" has the same meaning as "out of the frying pan and into the fire." Or "some like meat, others prefer medicine" is like "one man's meat is another man's poison." And then there is the popular "when you visit the country where they blink their eyes, you must blink your eyes too." Of course that is the same as "when in Rome, do as the Romans do."

THE THAI ALPHABET

In 1283 Sukhothai's greatest king, Ramkhamhaeng, set up a stone monument with an inscription honoring his reign. On it was a new alphabet, inspired by and yet different from the Khmer alphabet, the oldest example of written Thai. Like Khmer, the Thai alphabet is based on the Tamil alphabet of South India.

In Ramkhamhaeng's inscription, both consonants and vowels were written on the same line. Eventually this system was changed so that only consonants were written on the line, vowels being written off the line. At present, Thai write their vowels either before, after, above, or below the consonants. This creates difficulties in setting type for publishers of print media and in locating dictionary listings.

The Thai language has 44 consonants, representing 20 consonant sounds, and 32 vowels. There are four tonal marks (midtone is never indicated). Written Thai is read from left to right, like English, and there are no spaces

Students during a class. The vast majority of the Thai population is literate.

between words within the same sentence, a factor that certainly makes it difficult for those learning to read Thai.

MEANING IN THAI NAMES

There are tens of thousands of Thai names, and every one has a meaning. Names commonly include words such as *porn* (porn), meaning "blessing"; *boon* (boon), meaning "merit"; *siri* (SEE-rih), meaning "glory"; *som* (sorm), meaning "fulfillment"; *thang* (tahng), meaning "gold"; and *thawee* (TAH-wee), meaning "increase."

As many as 3,000 names are used for both men and women. But as a general rule, parents name boys after strength or honor, and girls are named for "feminine" qualities—such as beauty and purity—or after flowers, plants, and fruit. Given names are not ordinarily used. Instead people go by a nickname given early in life, either because of some obvious physical quality such as height and color of complexion or because of a personality trait. Examples are *moo* (moo), meaning "pig"; *noo* (noo), meaning "mouse" or "rat"; and *dueng* (dwang), meaning "red."

Surnames are rarely used. King Rama VI introduced them as part of his own Westernization program, giving out many personally, including both Thai and Western spellings. Thai generally refer to one's surname the first time they meet somebody, then switch to using the given name.

Thai like to translate their names, letter by letter, into the romanized form used in the West. But since most Thai names have several silent letters, the romanized versions usually bear little resemblance to the way they are actually pronounced. This applies to surnames, first names, and names of streets, towns, and places. For example, King Chulalongkorn's name is pronounced "Ju-lah-long-gohrn." And if you think that's difficult, try *Dasaneeyavaja*. It is pronounced "Tah-sah-nee-YAH-wed." Sometimes the exact Thai sound just cannot be pronounced in English.

Children at a streetside market outside Nat Thon. Most Thai use a nickname given early in life.

We call it Bangkok. Thai call it Krung Thep, but that's a drastic reduction. Its full name, consisting of 167 Thai letters, is Krung Thep Mahanakhon Amon Rattanakosin Mahinthara Yuthaya Mahadilok Phop Noppharat Ratchathani Burirom Udomratchaniwet Mahasathan Amon Piman Awatan Sathit Sakkathattiya Witsanukam Prasit.

Translated it means "City of Angels, Great City of Immortals, Magnificent Jeweled City of the God Indra, Seat of the King of Ayutthaya, City of Gleaming Temples, City of the King's Most Excellent Palace and Dominions, Home of Vishnu and All the Gods."

Bangkok was not always known by this name; before it became Thailand's capital in 1782, it was just a tiny village by the Chao Phraya and was called Bang Makok. Bang (bahng) *means "riverside village," and* makok (mah-KAWK) *means "olive" or a kind of plum.*

BODY LANGUAGE

Words, of course, are not the sole tool of communication in Thai. Thai also use a range of gestures and motions, from the obvious *wai* to more subtle movements that constitute a recognizable body language. This is used to add meaning to the spoken word as well as to show respect or indicate one's place in society.

The head is a sacred part of the body. The *khwan* living in the head may leave if it is touched and only return after a special ritual. Except for lovers, Thai people do not touch one another's heads.

Moreover, in any social encounter or gathering, the head of the highest-ranking person should always be above everyone else's. In practice, this is nearly impossible to arrange, so lower-ranked people sit with their shoulders slumped or their heads lowered. In the presence of monks, Thai consider it inappropriate to sit with their legs crossed.

The general taboos surrounding rowdy behavior include laughing in a loud, unruly way, elbowing, kicking, and shouting. Thai will point with a finger at a lifeless object but never at people. Instead they will use a verbal description or, if more is needed, a slight jerk of the chin in the direction of the person in question. They frown on any public display of affection. In fact, conservative behavior is seen as a sign of maturity.

Thai try to keep their hands as still as possible during conversations. They do not nudge each other to attract attention or to make a point. However, when beckoning servants and waiters, Thai may wave with their hands. They do so rapidly, bringing the fingers to the forearm.

In Thai culture the left hand is customarily used to clean the body. Thus, Thai always use the right hand when passing something to someone. If an inferior is passing something to a superior, he or she uses the left hand to support the right forearm. Women never pass anything directly to monks.

INTERNET LINKS

http://thaiarc.tu.ac.th/thai/peansiri.htm

This website provides an interesting discussion that was presented to a workshop of teachers of social science organized by the University of New Orleans.

www.omniglot.com/writing/thai.htm

This website specializes in the writing system of the Thai language, featuring its origins, the Thai alphabet, Thai numerals, vowel diacritics, tone indication, punctuation, and more.

www.thai-language.com/

This is a valuable Internet resource for those wishing to learn the Thai language. There are audio clips, dictionary entries, images, and illustrations. It is suitable for English speakers with any level of interest— from beginners who wish to learn a few useful vacation phrases to advanced students who are preparing to live or work in Thailand.

ARTS

An artist painting parasols at the Bo Sang handicraft village.

10

THE FIRST THAI EFFORTS AT storytelling were folktales told by authors whose identities have been lost in the mists of time. In the past, when there were few literate people, these stories were recited at the *wat* during the Buddhist Lent.

Today this custom survives only in Nakhon Si Thammarat in the south and at Bangkok's Temple of the Emerald Buddha. Nowadays people can read these stories for themselves.

Thailand's folktales have their share of animal heroes, clever rogues, stupid tigers, lucky younger brothers, monsters, and ogres. But the most popular tales are those featuring supernatural feats, romantic adventurers, and typically beautiful and helpless heroines.

The first important works of literature date back to King Borommatrailokkanat's reign (1448—88), when religious works such as *Lilit Phra Law* and the *Mahachat* (the Prince Vessandorn story) were composed. Classical Thai poetry written at this time included a heavy dose of Sanskrit or Pali words.

Classical literature peaked just before Ayutthaya's fall. Under the patronage of royalty and nobility, Thai art flourished in the hands of writers, sculptors, painters, dancers, architects, and skilled craftsmen.

LITERARY KINGS

Nearly all copies of early Thai literary works were lost in the destruction of Ayutthaya. King Rama I, himself an accomplished poet, then called on the memories of old scholars and teachers who had survived Ayutthaya's fall and asked them to re-create such Thai classics as the *Ramakien*, the epic tale concerned with the life and adventures of the legendary King Ramachandra and his wife, Sita, and *Khun Chang Khun Phaen*, a Siamese love story.

Both tales provided the basis for dance-dramas and other performing arts. The best of the early tales were written by King Rama II (1767—1824)—an even better poet than his father—and his contemporary Sunthorn Phu (1786—1855), considered Thailand's greatest classical writer. Rama II also created a dance-drama version of *Inao*, a Javanese romantic poem, whereas *Phra Abhai Mani*, an adventure through real and imaginary seas, is Sunthorn Phu's masterpiece. Another notable literary figure was Rama VI, who was a very prolific writer. He composed poems and essays and was also the first Thai king to be educated in the West. He was a student of Shakespearean literature and translated some of it into Thai. He also translated French dramas and wrote several modern plays. More than anyone else, he is credited with introducing new literary forms to Thai writing.

Modern Thai literature spans a wide range of topics. Some are historical works, such as the late prime minister Kukrit Pramoj's *Four Reigns*, a novel drawing material from the court of Rama V to that of Rama VIII. Other important modern authors include Phya Anuman Rajadhon, M. L. Bubpha Nimmanahaeminda (who used the pseudonym Dokmaisod), and Lao Khamhom (Khamsing Srinawk). Phya Anuman Rajadhon published numerous works on Thai heritage, language, and traditions. Dokmaisod's books are widely studied in high schools and universities throughout Thailand. Lao Khamhom's books deal largely with present-day social problems of both rural and urban people, political corruption, and class differences.

BUDDHIST ARCHITECTURE

Within each Buddhist temple compound are several buildings and monuments. The largest room in Thai temples is the *bot* (boht), a rectangular hall with a high pointed roof where chanting and ordinations take place. The next largest room is the *viharn* (vee-HAHN), where rituals are staged.

On a platform high off the ground stands the library, where old texts are stored. There may also be a small crematorium, recognizable by the tall chimney. The other buildings house the monks.

Temple compounds contain one or more *chedi* (CHAY-dee). These are spirelike monuments with broad bases and slender tops that either rise like a rounded-off column or taper to a point. The oldest of these are simple in design. Newer ones, such as that of the 16th-century Wat Po in Bangkok, have ornate decorations running the length of the monument.

Chedi were originally ritual objects made to store gold and silver. Sometimes they were covered with these precious metals. For example, the entire *chedi* of Wat Haripunchai in Lamphun is plated with gold. *Chedi*, however, attracted thieves and foreign armies; armies wanting the gold that was inside the kingdom's *chedi* destroyed ancient Ayutthaya to get to it.

Decorations were a fine art in the temple compounds. Wood-carvers created jungle scenes on doors, window shutters, eaves, and posts. Sculptors made Buddhas and gods in various sizes and all sorts of poses.

Other craftsmen fashioned chipped-glass decorations or supplied special textiles, such as the long, thin banners used in ceremonies. Religious and historical murals found inside the *viharn* or the *bot* reveal much about Thailand in centuries gone by, from clothing design to the appearance of gods, heroes, demons, enemy soldiers, and curious European adventurers.

The Buddhist temples in Thailand boast beautiful architecture with intricate and elaborate detailing such as that of Wat Rong Khun, also known as the White Temple.

PERFORMING ARTS

The most fascinating art form developed under the early Chakri kings was the dance-drama. Produced by royalty, dance-drama performances today are lavish.

A dancer performance with some dancers wearing masks. Many performers have done away with masks.

There are two traditional types of dance-drama: the *khon* (kohn) and the *lakon* (la-KOHN). Originally all *khon* performers were masked, except for those playing goddesses and women. Present-day actors playing gods and men have also discarded their masks. These performers put on crowns or headdresses instead, whereas those portraying animals and demons remain masked.

Both vocal and instrumental music—the latter played on the lutelike *phipat* (PEE-paht)—accompanies the action. There is a chorus in the cast as well. Dancers use gestures that are elegant versions of those used in daily life. The performers dance to stories woven around episodes from the *Ramakien*.

Lakon nok dramas are lively and fast-paced, with lots of rough humor. *Lakon nai* are the opposite—poetic and graceful, tender, with slow music, and no vulgarity. Episodes from the *Inao* are commonly performed; other Thai classics and tales imported from India, less so. Scenery, now vital to any staging of dance-dramas, is a 20th-century innovation.

Music and dance flourished under Rama VI. After his reign ended in 1925, the Great Depression affected royal sponsorship, and there were few shows. Responsibility for the troupes and orchestras was transferred to the government after 1934, only to be forgotten. But with the end of World War II, the government sponsored a revival, and a host of new dancers and actors were trained. Some even performed independently. Most dances are performed by women in gorgeous costumes with props such as candles, long attached fingernails, gossamer wings, and elaborate crowns and headdresses.

The *likay* (LEE-kay) is the Thai version of commedia dell'arte, or professional group comedy. The *likay* originated in Bangkok in the 1880s. It uses song and dialogue, both of which are often vulgar, with a collection of stock characters and situations. The *likay* is usually performed without a script.

OTHER THEATRICAL ARTS

Another kind of traditional theater replaces actors with puppets. In the south, shadow plays similar to those of Malaysia and Indonesia depict stories from

A *Hun Lakhon Lek* performance is one that uses puppets instead of actors.

the *Ramakien* by casting shadows from leather figures onto a screen. In other places, wooden puppets—the kind of puppet more familiar in the rest of the world—take the roles.

Thai Chinese have their own type of puppets and plays with plots from Chinese classics. They also have their traditional operas, which feature spectacular costumes, familiar plots, and music with the emphasis on gongs and drums. Chinese operas are regularly staged in Bangkok. In coastal towns, operas are sometimes presented at a private house or an open park, free to all who wish to attend.

A Chinese opera performance.

Traditional Thai orchestras accompany theater presentations. Instruments include cymbals, xylophones, three-string lutes, bass fiddles, and bass drums. Large reed pipes may also be a part of the orchestra, especially in the northeast. Songs mark the rhythm by use of pitch accents instead of beats as in Western music.

HILL SONGS

Hill groups fashioned many of their traditional musical instruments from materials found in the nearest patch of jungle. Bamboo is perfect for making flutes, Jew's harps, oboes, and both large and small gourd pipes.

The hill people carve their stringed instruments and two sizes of drums from wood. They use buffalo hide to cover the drums and make music out of buffalo horns. Bells and gongs complete the collection of instruments.

Hill music has its own repertoire of love songs and sad songs. But among hill groups, these songs are often more than mere entertainment. Mothers pass on much of the culture through carefully worded lullabies. Other songs

A band using traditional Insan instruments: a hand drum and a reed-free bamboo mouth organ known as the *khaen*.

tell children how to behave around adults. Some songs sung during certain festivals help to reinforce cultural values.

The Akha have perhaps the greatest body of songs in the hills. Some are in ancient Akha, and even those who sing them do not know what all the words mean. Some are accompanied by dances performed in the Akha dancing ground.

Other groups generally dance only at big festivals, usually with friends and relatives, and often in circles.

WEAVING

Thai weavers have produced some of the world's most beautiful fabrics. Most of the best are kept by the weavers themselves to be worn on special occasions. The fanciest fabrics have, over the years, become collectors' items. In the past, girls in the north and the northeast had to know how to weave in order to get married.

Thailand produces some of the most beautiful silk in the world. Included among the fans of Thai silk have been the United States' former first lady Eleanor Roosevelt, cosmetics queen Helena Rubinstein, and Britain's Queen Elizabeth II. In the movies *Ben-Hur* and *The King and I*, Thai silk was used to make the stars' costumes. Even airlines have used this silk to decorate the interiors of their planes.

Thailand's silk industry was dying out until it caught the eye of Jim Thompson, a former World War II American intelligence officer who was already a lover of Thai art. Directly supervising the work and introducing new color schemes, Thompson—who was called the "father of modern Thai silk"—built Thai silk into a glamorous export appreciated around the world. His disappearance in 1967 during a forest walk in Malaysia is an unsolved mystery that has increased his legendary status.

Thai cultivate both cotton and silk, and they are masters at the complex and delicate method of turning these into quality thread. Traditionally they dyed thread with local plants—indigo particularly—or substances produced by insects, such as lac. Sometimes Thai weavers tie the threads into patterns before dyeing in a process known as *matmee* (MUT-mee).

The typical loom is a wood-frame handloom with four harnesses with heddles (vertical cords through which the thread is drawn), four treadles, and a bench to sit on. It can produce cloth that is about 3 feet (0.9 m) wide and of any length. The Karen use the simpler backstrap loom, whereas the Akha and the Meo operate a narrow, stand-up, bamboo-frame loom. Most weaving takes place in the winter, the slack time in the rural year.

The most complex, eye-catching patterns of Thai clothing are embroidered. This can be done on the loom by adding a set of heddle sticks to lift the different warp threads to allow another weft thread to make the design. Both the Thai on their big looms and the Karen on their small ones do this extremely well. Northern weavers sometimes create patterns of animals and religious symbols on banners.

The other way to add embroidery is to stitch it on a finished piece, the way the Meo, the Akha, and the Yao do it. Women from these groups spend their spare time embroidering clothes for themselves and their families. Most are familiar with a range of their own traditional patterns, but they have been borrowing designs lately, thanks to greater contact with one another.

AKHA JACKETS

While chatting, feeding a baby, or even walking to the fields, an Akha woman's hands are always busy. Much of her time is spent embroidering her beautiful jackets. Using bold colors—the more the better—against a deep blue or black cloth, she works on patterns with names such as "river flow" or the exotic "butterfly lips." After finishing the piece, she decorates it with a range of materials, including seeds, beads, cowries, silver coins and studs, monkey fur, beetle wings, and tassels of horsetail or chicken feathers.

SCULPTURE AND PAINTING

Prior to the Sukhothai period, three main sculptural styles existed in Thailand. The oldest, of the Mon in the Dvaravati period, shows a strong Indian influence. The second, of the Mahayana Buddhist kingdom of Srivijaya, became popular in the eighth century. The subjects were mainly the Buddha and bodhisattvas, humanlike with full Indian faces representing grace and strength.

The third style, from the Khmer period, developed during the 10th century. This style featured realistic sculptures of ethnic, non-Indian personalities. These are quite masculine but friendly and gentle-looking. Many of the images are of Hindu gods.

During the Sukhothai period, another style developed. Statues of Hindu gods were still being made, but the Sukhothai contribution was to create a different, very Thai representation of the Buddha, with a slender, idealized body and often a dreamy smile. Sukhothai sculptors also created a new form, the walking Buddha, perfected in grace and elegance. Thai sculpture since Sukhothai essentially repeats and refines the forms of the original masters.

Until recently Thai craftsmen sculpted and painted only for the temples or for royalty. Modern sculptors, like today's painters, have trouble finding business as well as establishing a new style. Thai temple murals are a fascinating blend of the real with the fantastic, but modern painters sometimes move from symbolic art to more realistic, illustrative art, which depicts objects as they appear.

HANDICRAFTS

Traditionally handicrafts were not for display but for use. Decorations were added for show. Thailand's antiques shops are full of interesting surprises, as younger Thai with different values sell off their family antiques. If it were not for tourism, many handicraft skills would have died out years ago. Unlike in the past, Thai craftspeople today produce art mainly for sale.

BASKETRY The traditional house needed all sorts of baskets to store clothing, rice, tobacco, and betel leaves. Bamboo, rattan, teak, and rosewood were the most frequently used materials for making baskets.

LACQUERWARE Elegant lacquered boxes were used to store various items. Lacquered boards or boards of ivory or niello (a black metal) were sometimes used as book covers.

PEWTER Pewter is a tin-based material used for making bowls, goblets, cups, and other objects.

JEWELRY Thai love gold and precious stones. Rubies, jade, and amber come from Myanmar but are often cut in Bangkok. Hill groups favor chunky silver ornaments and jewelry from forest materials.

CERAMICS Water jars and smaller water pots—the latter placed in front of houses for passersby—are common. Fired pale-green stoneware, called celadon, is the most refined of all ceramics.

A potter at work in Nonthaburi.

VASAN SITTHIKET

Vasan Sitthiket is one of Thailand's most prolific and well-known contemporary artists. Born in 1957 in Nakhon Sawan, he studied at the College of Fine Art in Bangkok. The main themes of his work relate to current problems in Thai society, including the gap between the wealthy and the poor as well as corruption in Thai political circles. He works in various media, producing paintings, drawings, woodcut prints, installations, and performances to express his ideas. He also writes poetry, children's fiction, and political works. Vasan has exhibited widely at home in Thailand and internationally in places such as Japan, Singapore, Seoul, and further afield in Italy for the Venice Biennale in 2003.

INTERNET LINKS

www.seameo.org/vl/thailifearts/artscrafts.htm

This website is maintained by the Southeast Asian Ministers of Education Organization (SEAMEO). It covers the folk arts and crafts of Thailand, including lacquerware, silverware, wood carving, embroidery, basketry, silk making, and more.

http://thailandculturecustomguide.org/thai-culture-customs/traditional-performing-arts.html

This website provides detailed information on the traditional performing arts in Thailand, including dancing and singing, usefully categorized by region.

www.thaifolk.com/Doc/literate_e.htm

This website features traditional tales and legends from Thailand, including discussions on their meaning, characteristics, and importance.

LEISURE

A girl from the Karen hill tribe playing with a soccer ball.

11

THAI HAVE A TRADITION OF contests of strength and skill. In earlier days the most impressive display was the ancient Mon sport of sword fighting. Opponents held two swords and fought with eye-blurring precision. A similar combat was also staged with sticks.

Nowadays a more popular entertainment is Muay Thai, or Thai kickboxing. This is different from ordinary boxing in that fighters not only throw punches but kick as well. Thai kickboxing originated during

Thai enjoy a diverse range of leisure and entertainment activities, from the unique sport of Thai kickboxing to the more universal activities of golf and shopping.

Boxers at a Muay Thai studio.

the Ayutthaya period, when it was taught as a means of self-defense. Today it is a spectator sport. Kickboxing champions are popular heroes to their fans.

Thai boxing fans also like to follow the fortunes of famous Western boxers. Thailand regularly produces world-champion boxers, usually in the lightweight divisions of the World Boxing Association. Any internationally televised championship fight is likely to interrupt all work as the men gather round to cheer on their favorite contestants.

Boys playing soccer on a beach. Soccer is a very popular game in Thailand.

Next to kickboxing and boxing, soccer is the most popular competitive sport. School games are heavily supported, and the triumphs and defeats of the national team in international matches are closely followed.

ANIMAL COMBAT

Cockfighting is one of the Thai's favorite pastimes, especially during the lull after the January rice harvest. Many Thai in the rural areas take cockfighting very seriously. Owners raise fighting cocks separately from other chickens. Once they are eight months old, the chicks are mixed with adult cocks and trained for mortal combat.

Fights are usually held in small circular stadiums. The cocks are blindfolded. Just before the fight begins, their owners put metal spurs on their feet. The cocks are released, and they claw at each other until one dies. Heavy gambling accompanies each round, along with cheering and shouting.

Near these same arenas, there are often small aquariums containing fish the size of a child's finger. These are the famous Thai fighting fish, which nudge and push each other. Spectators gather to place their bets on which fish will win the fight while cheering on their favorites.

In hillside villages children go around looking for armored horned beetles. They capture these beetles and tie them onto a stick. The children position two beetles so that they face each other. By prodding them with a straw, the children induce the insects to lock horns and wrestle.

GAMES

Board games of various kinds are popular with the older generation. Thai chess is known as *makruk* (mak-ROOK) and originated in Cambodia. *Makruk* resembles Chinese chess, though with 64 squares as in Western chess, but the moves are different from either.

Among Thai royalty, checkers, polo, and *rua pung* (ROO-ah poong) are favorite games. A *rua pung* is a ball of lead, and the game is played on a field 132 feet (40 m) long and only 3 feet (0.9 m) wide, enclosed by banana trees and filled with sand or rice-paddy husks. The object is to see who can hurl the *rua pung* the farthest and straightest downfield.

Gambling with dice, cards, or other things has always been a common pastime. These games provide players with good company and cheap entertainment, no matter what happens to their money.

Thai children have their own games. In one, known as *ee-tak* (ee-TAHK), or the scoop game, they try to pick up fruit seeds one at a time from a pile using a special paper scoop without disturbing the other seeds. Another popular game is "snake eats its tail," where two of the strongest children play the father and mother snakes. The rest play baby snakes and form a chain behind the mother snake. The object is for the "mother" to prevent the "father" from catching the "babies."

SPORTS AND EXERCISE

Early each morning, Bangkok's Lumphini Park is crowded with office workers and other professionals jogging or doing tai chi, gymnastics, or other forms of exercise. Even the provincial towns have parks that are filled with joggers every morning and evening.

One simple, popular game is *takraw* (TAH-krohr). Players gather in a wide circle and kick or head a ball made of strips of rattan. The players

Players of *sepak takraw* display great agility.

have to keep the ball from hitting the ground. A later development of this simple game was the addition in the 1930s of a high basket. The object of the game then was to send the ball through the basket, with points scored according to the difficulty of the shot.

Teams compete on either side of a net in *sepak takraw* (SAY-pahk TAH-krohr). The rules and scoring are like those in volleyball, except players can use only their feet and are allowed to freely change positions.

Kite fights are held annually. These kites are shaped like a star, without tails. A jerk of the string is enough to send the kite flying. Competitors win if their kites "capture" other kites by entangling and sawing off the strings of the other kites. Much gambling goes on during these kite fights.

RECREATION

The Thai word for fun is *sanuk* (sah-NOOK), and a good sense of *sanuk* fills the atmosphere both at work and at play. Interpreting the word more broadly, it means having a cheerful, carefree attitude toward entertainment and games at any social gathering. Being a friendly and sociable people, Thai always go out in groups, and the company is usually every bit as much *sanuk* as the event itself.

Thai have a great variety of leisure options. There are golf courses and nature parks throughout the country, health spas, and snooker (a game similar to pool) halls in every town—there are 800 snooker halls in Bangkok alone. There is also a wide range of travel agencies offering domestic or international tour packages.

Islands and beaches are favorite haunts, especially on weekends when students and executives have some free time on their hands. Boating, windsurfing, snorkeling, diving, and parasailing are among the most popular water sports.

ENTERTAINMENT

In earlier times, people flocked to watch marionette shows, theater performances, or acrobatic acts featuring artistes on 20-foot (6-m) poles.

People amuse themselves differently nowadays. Most urbanites have easy access to the Internet and own a television. Almost everyone has a radio.

The cinema is another popular form of entertainment. Martial-arts movies—especially Hong Kong productions dubbed in Thai—and love-triangle sagas seem to be the most popular among the Thai viewership.

The nightlife is quite active in some cities, such as Pattaya and Phat Phong. Most nightclubs, bars, and lounges stay open past midnight, as do restaurants. In a typical Thai cocktail lounge, there will usually be a female singer and a backup band—not much different from lounges in the West.

Shopping malls, night markets, and streetside dining places are also entertainment spots for Thai; people watching and window-shopping are common pastimes in Thailand, as in many other places in the world.

INTERNET LINKS

www.muaythaionline.org/links/thaiboxing.html

This website provides information about Thai kickboxing, or Muay Thai, including the sport's history and techniques, as well as links to other useful websites.

www.sportsthailand.net/

Thailand's leading sports website serves to connect sports fans throughout Thailand. The site also promotes sports events, groups, forums, and videos.

www.thai-blogs.com/2009/08/19/thai-cock-fighting-festival/?blog=5

This website provides an interesting personal account of a Thai cockfighting festival, including photographs and a video link.

FESTIVALS

Paper streamers adding color to the festivities of
the Songkran Festival.

12

THE BIRTHDAYS OF THE KING AND queen of Thailand are important national holidays.

Schools and government offices are carefully decorated, and the area around the Grand Palace in Bangkok is lit up spectacularly and graced by fireworks. Two days before the king's birthday, the colorful Royal Guards troop by the royal family to renew their oath of loyalty.

With less pomp, Thai also honor Chakri Day—celebrating the founding of the current dynasty—and Coronation Day, which marks the rise of King Bhumibol to the crown. King Chulalongkorn's achievements are acknowledged on another day, on which people lay wreaths before his statue.

Previously the king personally took part in the royal plowing ceremony, a rite staged every April to announce the start of the planting season. But since the reign of King Mongkut, the king only attends the event while his delegate, usually the minister of agriculture, performs the ceremony by plowing three troughs. Following this ceremony, several prophecies are read and interpreted in various ways to the king.

TRADITIONAL THAI FESTIVALS

NATIONWIDE As a Buddhist country, Thailand celebrates important anniversaries with ceremonies that give Buddhists around the country an opportunity to do their part in merit-making. Many ceremonies are accompanied by gifts to monks and candlelit processions at night. Sometimes there are gatherings where religious tales are told.

Magha Puja in February marks the day 1,250 disciples assembled to hear the Buddha preach. And Visakha Puja in May celebrates the birth, enlightenment, and death of the Buddha.

Khao Phansa in July announces the start of the Buddhist Lent, which is also the beginning of the annual monsoon retreat. It ends three months later with the Kathin ceremony, in which people give monks new robes.

In the traditional calendar, New Year falls on April 13. The Thai New Year, better known as Songkran, is an occasion not only for merit-making but also for enjoyment. This is the occasion when people go around dousing one another with water from cups, buckets, or hoses.

The most beautiful event of the year is Loy Krathong, held for three days during the full moon of November. *Krathong* (krah-TOHNG) are small candles or lamps mounted on floats made from leaves. During the nights of the celebration every stretch of water in Thailand is filled with thousands of candles inside beautiful little leaf baskets. In Chiang Mai, the tradition includes the release of giant hot-air balloons. Everywhere, processions, fireworks, and lights grace these three nights.

REGIONAL While everyone participates in the national festivals, many provinces have unique events of their own. Among the most interesting

Loy Krathong is from the legend of a beautiful and talented woman named Kang Noppamas, who made the first *krathong* 700 years ago. Honoring Mother Water in her own way, she presented the *krathong* to King Ramkhamhaeng, who accepted it, lit the candle in it, and launched it on the water.

Beautiful *krathong* floating on water during the Loy Krathong festival.

The start of the buffalo race in Chonburi.

regional festivals is Lampang's Luang Wiang Lakon in February, a procession of Buddhist images. Sometimes members of the former royal family of Chiang Mai participate in this event.

The rocket festival in Yasothon in the northeast involves the firing of homemade rockets of all sizes that people believe will ensure a good monsoon and an abundant harvest.

Loei's Phi Ta Khon in June is a merry celebration of Prince Vessandorn's return to his city. Everyone dresses as ghosts for the day.

Every September low-slung wooden boats race on the Nan River in Phichit.

During Surat Thani's Chak Phra celebration in October, Buddha images are mounted on carriages and hauled through the streets and floated on rivers and canals.

At the buffalo races in Chonburi in October, farmers' most valuable animals participate in parades and races.

Sakon Nakhon's Wax Castle Festival in October sees the making of beautiful miniature temples in beeswax.

The racing of brightly painted wooden boats in Lanna, Nan, every October accompanies the giving of robes to local monks.

CHINESE FESTIVALS

Thailand's Chinese population celebrates the Lunar New Year in late January or early February. Merchants take a rest, offices close for several days, and all sorts of decorations go up. Loud noise is the hallmark of the celebration, along with the burning of banknotes, fireworks, and processions.

Large Chinese communities around the country also stage lion and dragon dances. The most spectacular displays are held at Nakhon Sawan, where the Chinese honor the Golden Dragon deity for his benevolence to them with a grand parade.

Chinese immigrants in Phuket and Trang celebrate the unusual annual Vegetarian Festival. This has become the event of the year in these cities. During this celebration the Chinese go on a 10-day vegetarian diet and stage many parades. They also perform amazing feats, such as walking across a bed of burning coals and piercing their faces with sharp steel rods. The participants enter a trance during these performances and show no signs of pain.

A Taoist priestess in traditional dress saying prayers during the Vegetarian Festival.

OTHER FESTIVALS

MUSLIM Ramadan is the most important event in the Islamic calendar. Muslims fast from sunrise to sunset for one month and go to the mosque for religious studies in the evenings. A great feast called Eid ul-Fitr marks the end of the period. Muslims also observe Hijra Day, which commemorates the Prophet Mohammed's trip to the city of Medina, Saudi

One of the most dangerous rites of Thailand's traditional festivals used to be the Giant Swing in Bangkok. The swing was attached to a wooden frame 60 feet (18.3 m) high. In a ceremony that welcomed the Indian gods Phra Isuan (also known as Shiva) and Phra Narai (also known as Vishnu), a young Indian devotee would ride the Giant Swing to seize, with his teeth, a moneybag hung in front of the frame. The devotees risked life and limb to collect bags that contained only 8-12 baht each. In 1935 the Giant Swing was taken out of use because the support beams were no longer strong enough to hold the men. In 2006, however, it was reconstructed. The timbers of the original swing are preserved in the National Museum. Today the swing stands in front of Wat Suthat, and many tourists visit this religious structure in Bangkok.

Arabia, and the start of the Islamic year. In addition, Muslims observe the Haj, the traditional annual pilgrimage to Mecca.

MON The Mon of Samut Prakan, south of Bangkok, celebrate their own Songkran with a thorough housecleaning, processions, and various rites, including setting birds and fishes free.

SHAN Shan, the majority group in Mae Hong Son, perform the Poy Sang Long ceremony in April. Young novices about to enter monkhood are dressed in beautiful clothing and carried through town.

A group of girls from the Akha hill tribe gather for a festival.

FESTIVALS OF THE HILL GROUPS

All hill people celebrate New Year's Day, though not necessarily on the same day. For example, the Karen, the Lisu, and the Yao observe it on the same day as the Chinese, and most Yao rites closely resemble Chinese practices. Other groups such as the Akha and the Meo hold their New Year's Day a month or so earlier. The slaughtering of animals, rounds of lavish feasting and drinking, and lots of singing and dancing characterize the event.

On New Year's Day young boys spin tops, hurling them against their opponents' tops to knock them out of competition. Among the hill people, New Year's Day is the beginning of the courting season, so young men and women dress up to show off. Meo youths line up opposite one another and toss balls back and forth—a perfect opportunity for introductions. Akha adolescents beat bamboo drums together throughout the night. The Lisu dance in small groups around the village priest's tree to the music of gourd pipes and lutes.

OFFICIAL THAI HOLIDAYS

New Year's Day	January 1
Magha Puja	February
Chakri Day	April 6
Songkran	April 13
Visakha Puja	May
Royal Ploughing Ceremony	May
Khao Phansa	July
Queen's Birthday	August 12
Chulalongkorn Day	October 23
Loy Krathong	November
King's Birthday	December 5
Constitution Day	December 10
New Year's Eve	December 31

Hill people stage many other ceremonies. These include rituals to start the rice-planting season, to bless the fall harvest, and to please guardian spirits or the invisible lords of the land, whom they consider the real owners of their rice fields.

The oldest women in Karen villages preside over a yearly ritual to please the spirits of their ancestors. The Meo hold one for the door spirit and another for the spirit of the central house post. Every year the Yao beg for forgiveness from the mountain spirit for allowing their animals to graze freely on its land.

Bad spirits must be kept out of the village area. So each September, Akha boys make wooden swords to chase them out, dashing through the houses in the villages. The Lisu trick the spirits into going to a feast that they hold outside the village boundary. A line of defensive taboo signs acts like a talisman, preventing the spirits from crossing the boundary and entering the village.

Elephants at the annual Surin elephant roundup getting ready for a game of soccer.

Many of these festivals are governed by a set of community rules. Rules commanding villagers to participate in a communal feast assure every family of a portion of protein-rich meat.

MAKING NEW FESTIVALS

With their love of *sanuk*, Thai invent festivals for anything and everything. Civic groups and business organizations support these festivals. The usual program includes displays, exhibits, entertainment programs of various sorts, processions, maybe a parade of floats, and definitely a beauty contest. The most famous of the newer festivals is the elephant roundup in Surin in the northeast. This festival has its origins in the 1960s and is an authentic reenactment of how wild elephants were once captured and trained. Both working and war elephants are used during the event.

The Tourism Authority of Thailand plays a key role in promoting the various local product fairs. Among them are festivals featuring the umbrellas of Bor Sang, the flowers of Chiang Mai, the straw birds of Chainat, and the silk of Khon Kaen. Fruit fairs are held in Rayong, Trat, Chanthaburi, and Nakhon Pathom, whereas specific fairs are held for the mango in Chachoengsao, the grape at Ratchaburi, the lychee at Chiang Rai, the rambutan at Surat Thani, the longan at Lamphun, the banana at Kamphaeng Phet, the *langsat* (LAHNG-saht) at Uttaradit, and the custard apple at Nakhon Ratchasima.

BEAUTY CONTESTS

Thai love beauty contests. Winners of major pageants are always front-page news in Thailand. Many become instant celebrities.

When Apasra Hongsakula was crowned Miss Universe in 1965, the country erupted into celebration. Her crowning revealed to much of the world, for the first time, the beauty of Thai women.

Two decades later, Thailand again went wild when Porntip Nakhirunkanok was crowned Miss Universe 1988. She was called a "national heroine." Even the government congratulated her and assigned her diplomatic duties.

Besides the national Miss Thailand pageant and its provincial semifinals, every festival in Thailand has a beauty contest or two. Every year someone is chosen as Miss Thailand World, Mrs. Thailand, Miss Farmer's Daughter, Miss Umbrella, Miss Mango, Miss Grape, Miss Longan, Miss Banana, Miss Lychee, and even Miss Transvestite!

INTERNET LINKS

www.thaifestivalblogs.com/festivals/index.php

This website is a comprehensive online guide to Thailand's many festivals. Details of dates, programs, and activities are provided for each of these major festivals, which are celebrated throughout the country.

www.thailandlife.com/thai-culture/king-chulalongkorn-the-great. html

This web page is dedicated to Chulalongkorn Day, with a brief explanation and photographs of the king and the celebration.

www.thailandlife.com/songkran-festival/index.php

This web page includes links to articles about Songkran, the traditional Thai New Year. These articles include "Origins of Songkran," "Songkran Water Fights," and "How to Celebrate Songkran."

www.tourismthailand.org/see-do/events-festivals/

Part of the official website of the Tourism Authority of Thailand, this page features a comprehensive calendar of events and festivals by date, category, and region.

The Red Cross Fair, held every January or February, is opened by Queen Sirikit, the Thai Red Cross's honorary president. The fair is filled with stalls operated by foreign embassies, Thai movie stars, various universities, and government departments. There is also classical and folk dancing as well as other entertainment. The money made at the fair is donated to the Red Cross.

FOOD

A woman selling produce at the Damnoen Saduak floating market.

13

THAI FOOD COMBINES ITS OWN indigenous recipes with Chinese and Indian culinary influences. The most famous Thai dishes are the spicy, seasoned stews and the smooth coconut curries.

Most meals use rice as the filler, but there are many noodle dishes and salads without rice. Ovens are not part of the ordinary Thai kitchen or small restaurant; food is either boiled or fried.

Thai food is never bland. The range of spices used includes chilies, pepper, coriander leaf and root, lemongrass, basil, ginger, mint, and screw pine. Sour soups are popular, and meat and fish are always served with sauces such as shrimp paste, tamarind, or honey with chili. Fish sauce is the basic substitute for salt across the country.

Thai cuisine uses a wide range of spices.

A woman cooking dinner in a traditional kitchen.

Spicy salads are a local specialty. They are made with raw prawns, meat, green papaya, field crab, or chopped raw meat, with a lot of chilies and other spices. Like the various noodle dishes, they are often sold at streetside stalls for those who want a light meal.

Thai have no food biases and are willing to try any sort of meat, wild or domestic, and most seafood. It is not unusual to see a menu offering dishes cooked with frog, snake, lizard, and deer.

A TRADITIONAL MEAL

Before visitors from the West introduced tables and chairs, Thai dined sitting on the floor around a small, low table. Various curries and other dishes were set on the table; these might be stir-fried cabbage and green bean and skewered or fried meat, crab, or fish. The hot, sour soup that is part of any full-course Thai meal was cooked in a clay pot that was placed in the center of the table.

Rice was served in small bowls to each person, who then used spoons or chopsticks to select pieces of food from the other bowls. Each diner also had a separate soup bowl that he or she filled from the common pot.

This traditional style of eating has not changed much; the only exception is that Thai now eat at a taller table. Soup is still placed in the center, if not in a clay pot then in a wheel-shape pan. But throughout the countryside, the old way still exists.

RICE

Several months of hard labor go into providing Thai diners with their most important food—rice. During the dry season, farmers have to break up the

A selection of rice on sale. Thai from different regions prefer to eat different types of rice.

hard ground and plough it when the first drops of rain arrive. Rice seedlings are planted in one part of the field, where they grow while the farmer cultivates and prepares another part of the field in which the rice will be transplanted at the start of the season of heavy rain.

Weeds and pests attack the rice fields all summer. Hoppers, rice bugs, field crabs, mice, and herons keep the farmers busy. After the rains comes the harvest, followed by the exhausting job of threshing, winnowing, and milling the rice grains.

Most Thai prefer the highly polished variety called *khao suai* (kaw sueye), or "beautiful rice." The people of Isan eat mainly sticky rice, or *khao nio* (kao neoh), as a staple, whereas most other Thai use *khao nio* in desserts. Northerners grow a different variety of rice that requires no transplanting and is milled just before cooking. This less polished rice is called *khao doi* (kao doy), or "mountain rice."

REGIONAL TASTES

ISAN The northeasterners in Isan serve their rice steamed and in sticky balls rolled by hand. The people of Isan eat these rice balls with dishes such as dried pork and beef jerky. Other Isan dishes include parts of animals that would not ordinarily be thought of as edible, such as the lungs and the lips. There are three sauces that accompany Isan meals: one bitter, one thick and spicy, and one thin, adorned with sliced chilies.

Children from a northern hill tribe watch their father prepare a meal in their home.

LANNA The people of this northern region like bamboo shoots in their dishes, with spiced raw beef, ox giblets, fermented ground pork, and Chiang Mai sausages. Cooks in Chiang Mai prepare these sausages with spices and lemongrass. *Kao soi* (kao soy), a Chiang Mai noodle curry, is a favorite snack.

THE SOUTH Sour curries with melon or morning glory are popular with the Thai living in the Malay Peninsula, along with fried seeds, rice-noodle curry, skewered meat with peanut sauce, and—with the sea on either side of the peninsula—all types of seafood, from shark steaks to cockles and mussels.

EXOTIC FOOD OF THE HILLS

Like traditional Thai, hill people sit around a low square or round table loaded with various dishes of curries, meat, and vegetables. Tables and bowls, plates and cups are all fashioned from bamboo and rattan. Chopsticks and spoons complete the utensils. A bit of alcohol made from distilled rice might come with the meal, especially during ceremonies.

People of the hill groups eat practically anything. Besides what they raise for themselves on their farms, they gather a great variety of edible plants, roots, brackens, and fruit from the jungles near their villages. In certain seasons they even gather insects such as bamboo grubs and wild bee larvae, which they consider good to eat.

Spring is the best hunting season. Hunters burn the fields to drive the animals out of the bushes. With snare traps, homemade long-barrel rifles, or even crossbows, hunters search for rabbits, deer, civets, monitor lizards, squirrels, wild boars, and bears. While working in the fields, they set traps to catch small birds, which they toss into a fire to both burn off the feathers and cook the meat.

During religious feasts the hill groups sacrifice animals including pigs (during weddings), buffalo (funerals), chickens (spirit or ancestor worship), and dogs (only in the Akha villages). The meat is usually divided equally among clan or village households.

INTERNET LINKS

www.guidetothailand.com/thailand-history/rice.php

This website features a fascinating article on the history of rice, the most important food in Thailand. It also presents a discussion on the spread of rice throughout Thailand and the region.

www.recipes4us.co.uk/Cooking%20by%20Country/Thailand.htm

This website provides culinary history, information, and recipes of Thailand. It features a discussion about ancient influences on Thai cuisine as well as an overview of Thai food today. The site also provides links to many recipes.

www.thai-food-online.co.uk/thairecipes.asp

This website provides downloadable Thai recipes with online video guides. Recipes include curries, starters, soups, salads, and sweets.

TOM YUM KUNG (HOT AND SOUR SHRIMP SOUP)

2 cups (500 ml) chicken broth

1 crushed clove of garlic

1 tablespoon (15 ml) minced lemongrass

1 tablespoon (15 ml) minced lime peel

3 tablespoons (45 ml) lime juice

1 1/2 tablespoons (22.5 ml) palm sugar or light brown sugar

1 1/2 tablespoons (22.5 ml) fish sauce

2 tablespoons (30 ml) chili-tamarind paste

1/3 pound (136 g) medium-size shrimp

3 ounces (85 g) sliced oysters or white mushrooms

3 tablespoons (45 ml) minced fresh cilantro

Combine chicken broth, garlic, lemongrass, and lime peel in a small saucepan over high heat and bring to a boil. After boiling for two minutes, stir in lime juice, sugar, fish sauce, and chili-tamarind paste until the soup is smooth. Add shrimp and oysters or mushrooms, and simmer for about two minutes, until the shrimp is fully cooked. Garnish with cilantro. Serve hot.

KHAO NIAOW MA MUANG
(THAI MANGO STICKY RICE DESSERT)

Serves 3—4

1 cup (250 ml) Thai sweet rice (also known as sticky rice)

water (for boiling or steaming the rice)

1 can good-quality (thick) coconut milk

pinch of salt

4 tablespoons (60 ml) palm sugar or brown sugar

1—2 ripe mangoes, cut into bite-size pieces

Soak the rice in a cup of water for at least 20 to 30 minutes in a saucepan. Add another ¾ cup of water and ¼ can of coconut milk, salt, and 1 tablespoon of sugar and stir the mixture together. Bring the mixture to a gentle boil and then reduce to medium to low heat. Partially cover the pot and leave it to simmer until the liquid has been absorbed by the rice. Take the pot off the heat but leave it to sit for another 5 to 10 minutes with the lid on.

In a separate pot, warm (do not bring to boil) the remaining coconut milk over low heat for about five minutes. Stir 3 tablespoons of sugar into the milk. Add scoops of rice into the sauce and break apart any large clumps of rice. Add the pieces of mango and continue stirring until entire mixture is warm. Portion into bowls and serve.

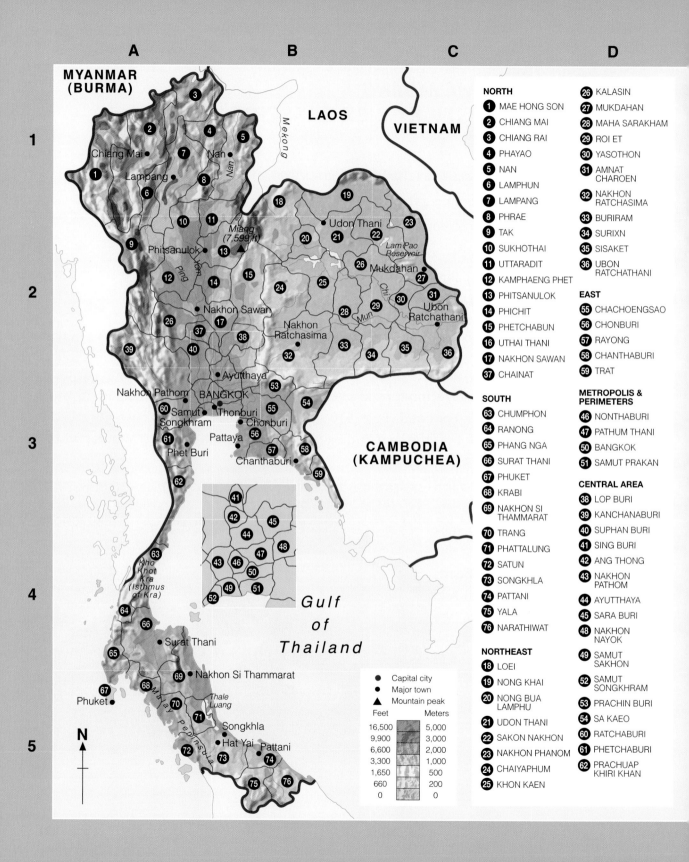

MYANMAR (BURMA)

LAOS

VIETNAM

A   **B**   **C**   **D**

1

2

3

4

5

Chiang Mai
Lampang
Nan
Phitsanulok
Miang
(7,599 ft)
Udon Thani
Lam Pao
Reservoir
Mukdahan
Nakhon Sawan
Nakhon
Ratchasima
Ubon
Ratchathani
Ayutthaya
Nakhon Pathom
BANGKOK
Samut
Songkhram
Thonburi
Chonburi
Pattaya
Phet Buri
Chanthaburi

CAMBODIA
(KAMPUCHEA)

Gulf
of
Thailand

Kho
Khot
Kra
(Isthmus
of Kra)

Surat Thani

Nakhon Si Thammarat

Phuket

Thale
Luang

Songkhla

Hat Yai

Pattani

Malay Peninsula

Ping
Yom
Nan
Mekong
Chi
Mun

N

NORTH	
1 MAE HONG SON	26 KALASIN
2 CHIANG MAI	27 MUKDAHAN
3 CHIANG RAI	28 MAHA SARAKHAM
4 PHAYAO	29 ROI ET
5 NAN	30 YASOTHON
6 LAMPHUN	31 AMNAT CHAROEN
7 LAMPANG	32 NAKHON RATCHASIMA
8 PHRAE	33 BURIRAM
9 TAK	34 SURIXN
10 SUKHOTHAI	35 SISAKET
11 UTTARADIT	36 UBON RATCHATHANI
12 KAMPHAENG PHET	
13 PHITSANULOK	**EAST**
14 PHICHIT	55 CHACHOENGSAO
15 PHETCHABUN	56 CHONBURI
16 UTHAI THANI	57 RAYONG
17 NAKHON SAWAN	58 CHANTHABURI
37 CHAINAT	59 TRAT

SOUTH

63 CHUMPHON
64 RANONG
65 PHANG NGA
66 SURAT THANI
67 PHUKET
68 KRABI
69 NAKHON SI THAMMARAT
70 TRANG
71 PHATTALUNG
72 SATUN
73 SONGKHLA
74 PATTANI
75 YALA
76 NARATHIWAT

METROPOLIS & PERIMETERS

46 NONTHABURI
47 PATHUM THANI
50 BANGKOK
51 SAMUT PRAKAN

CENTRAL AREA

38 LOP BURI
39 KANCHANABURI
40 SUPHAN BURI
41 SING BURI
42 ANG THONG
43 NAKHON PATHOM
44 AYUTTHAYA
45 SARA BURI
48 NAKHON NAYOK
49 SAMUT SAKHON
52 SAMUT SONGKHRAM
53 PRACHIN BURI
54 SA KAEO
60 RATCHABURI
61 PHETCHABURI
62 PRACHUAP KHIRI KHAN

NORTHEAST

18 LOEI
19 NONG KHAI
20 NONG BUA LAMPHU
21 UDON THANI
22 SAKON NAKHON
23 NAKHON PHANOM
24 CHAIYAPHUM
25 KHON KAEN

● Capital city
• Major town
▲ Mountain peak

Feet	Meters
16,500	5,000
9,900	3,000
6,600	2,000
3,300	1,000
1,650	500
660	200
0	0

MAP OF THAILAND

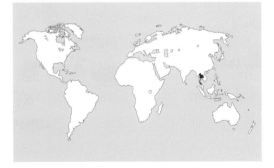

ECONOMIC THAILAND

Agriculture

🌾 Rice

🛢 Rubber

Manufacturing

🏭 Industrial hub

Natural Resources

🐟 Fish

💎 Gems

🛢 Oil and gas

T Tin

Services

✈ Airport

🚢 Port

🧳 Tourism

ABOUT THE ECONOMY

OVERVIEW

Thailand made an impressive recovery from the Asian financial crisis of 1997—98. During the period from 2000 to 2007 Thailand's economy grew an average of more than 4 percent annually. Its strong economy is supported by its high-performing export industries, first-class infrastructure, and a mainly laissez-faire economic policy that encourages investments. Thailand's economy, in particular its exports, suffered from the global financial crisis of 2008—09. Although the economy contracted by 2.2 percent in 2009, it made a powerful recovery in 2010, during which it grew 7.6 percent. This growth came despite antigovernment protests that hurt tourism as well as general business and consumer confidence in recent years, and the economy is expected to continue performing well into the foreseeable future.

GROSS DOMESTIC PRODUCT (GDP)

$586.9 billion (2010 est.)

ECONOMIC GROWTH RATE

7.6 percent (2010 est.)

CURRENCY

US$1 = THB 31.48 (January 2012)
1 baht (THB) = 100 satang

UNEMPLOYMENT RATE

1.2 percent (2010 est.)

INCOME PER CAPITA

$4,716 (2010 est.); $8,700 PPP (purchasing power parity)

MAJOR EXPORT TRADING PARTNERS

United States 10.9 percent, China 10.6 percent, Japan 10.3 percent, Hong Kong 6.2 percent, Australia 5.6 percent, Malaysia 5 percent (2009 est.)

MAJOR IMPORT TRADING PARTNERS

Japan 18.7 percent, China 12.7 percent, Malaysia 6.4 percent, United States 6.3 percent, UAE 5 percent, Singapore 4.3 percent, South Korea 4.1 percent (2009 est.)

MAJOR EXPORTS

Textiles and footwear, fishery products, rice, rubber, jewelry, automobiles, computers, electrical appliances

MAJOR IMPORTS

Capital goods, intermediate goods and raw materials, consumer goods, fuels

MAJOR PORTS AND HARBORS

Bangkok, Laem Chabang, Pattani, Phuket, Sattahip, Si Racha, Songkhla

INTERNATIONAL AIRPORTS

Bangkok, Hat Yai, Phuket, Chiang Rai, Chiang Mai

CULTURAL THAILAND

Chiang Saen
Famous for its ruins of the ancient Lanna Kingdom.

Lanna Orchid Ensemble
The Lanna Orchid Ensemble of the Chiang Mai University performs with instruments such as traditional fiddles, pipes, and lutes.

Sukhothai
The city of Sukhothai was founded in 1238 when the Thai wrestled for independence from Khmer rule.

Phra Pathom Chedi
Standing at 774 feet (236 m), the Phra Pathom Chedi in Nakhon Pathom is the tallest pagoda in the world. It is also the oldest Buddhist monument in Thailand; the pagoda dates back to the 4th century.

Shadow play house of Suchat Sapsin
The shadow play house of Suchat Sapsin in Nakhon Si Thammarat received the 1996 Thailand Tourism Award for the best cultural and historical site. Visitors are not only offered fascinating puppet performances, they get to see how shadow puppets are made.

Songkhla National Museum
Built in 1878, the museum was declared a National Monument in 1973. The museum building once served as the residence for Thai governors, state hall, and city hall before it became the National Museum in 1982.

Thai Elephant Conservation Centre
Since its establishment in 1969, the Thai Elephant Conservation Centre in Lampang has been a nursery for young elephants. Veterinarians from the Centre travel all over Thailand to treat sick elephants.

Ban Chiang Archaeological Site
Pottery, axes, and cloth woven from natural fibers left behind by prehistoric Thai settlers have been excavated from this site. These artifacts are approximately 3,500 years old.

Pha Taem National Park
The Pha Taem National Park in Ubon Ratchathan was founded in 1991. The park is famous for its prehistoric wall paintings.

Samut Prakarn Crocodile Farm
The Samut Prakarn Crocodile Farm in Bangkok is the largest crocodile farm in the world and is owned by none other than the Crocodile King of Thailand, Mr. Utai Youngprapakorn.

Temple of the Emerald Buddha
The temple in Bangkok is considered one of Thailand's holiest sites. The Buddha wears different costumes according to the seasons: a crown in the hot season, a golden shawl in the cool season, and a robe when it rains.

Wat Wai Suwannaram
This temple in Phetchaburi is built entirely from teak and houses murals of mythical angels. Some of these murals are 300 years old.

ABOUT THE CULTURE

OFFICIAL NAME
Kingdom of Thailand

DESCRIPTION OF NATIONAL FLAG
Five horizontal bands in red, white, and blue. Red stands for the nation and the blood of life, white represents religion and the purity of Buddhism, and blue represents the monarchy.

CAPITAL
Bangkok

POPULATION
66,720,153 (July 2011 est.)

ETHNIC GROUPS
Thai: 75 percent; Chinese: 14 percent; other: 11 percent (including Malay, Khmer, Mon, Shan, Karen, Hmong, Yao, Lahu, Akha, and Lisu)

RELIGION
Buddhist: 94.6 percent; Muslim: 4.6 percent; Christian: 0.7 percent; other: 0.1 percent

LANGUAGE
Thai

NATIONAL HOLIDAYS
New Year's Day (January 1); Chakri Day (April 6); Queen's Birthday (August 12); Chulalongkorn Day (October 13); King's Birthday (December 5); Constitution Day (December 10); New Year's Eve (December 31)

MAJOR NATIONWIDE FESTIVALS
Magha Puja (February); Songkran (April); Visakha Puja—Buddha's Birthday (May); Khao Phansa—Buddhist Lent (July); Loy Krathong (November)

IMPORTANT ANNIVERSARIES
June 24—day in 1932 when the Thai overthrew absolute monarchy and created a constitutional monarchy
October 14—day in 1973 when thousands of students marched in Bangkok to force the military dictatorship to resign

LITERACY RATE
92.6 percent

GREAT KINGS
Ramkhamhaeng—famous Sukhothai king
Rama I—founder of current Chakri Dynasty
Mongkut—king who first contacted the West
Chulalongkorn—regarded as the greatest king
Bhumibol Adulyadej—the current king

TIME LINE

IN THAILAND	IN THE WORLD

3500 B.C.
Ban Chiang settlements in northeastern Thailand are established.

1238
Thai establish a kingdom at Sukhothai; European nations compete for trade privileges.

1767
General Phraya Taksin governs Siam and moves the capital to Thonburi.

1782
General Chao Phraya Chakri becomes the first king of the dynasty and moves the capital to present-day Bangkok.

1827
War with Laos

1851
King Mongkut (Rama IV) begins trade reform and the modernization of the Thai education system.

1917
Siam joins the Allies in World War I.

1939
The nation of Siam is renamed Thailand.

1942
Thailand allies with Japan in World War II.

1944
Pro-Japanese government falls; Thailand joins the Allies.

1946
First postwar military government is established.

1973
Student revolution forces army out of power; three years later army regains control.

1980
Prem Tinsulanonda becomes prime minister; Thailand's economy grows rapidly.

1206–1368
Genghis Khan unifies the Mongols and starts conquest of the world. At its height, the Mongol Empire under Kublai Khan stretches from China to Persia and parts of Europe and Russia.

1776
U.S. Declaration of Independence

1789–99
The French Revolution

1914
World War I begins.

1939
World War II begins.

1945
The United States drops atomic bombs on Hiroshima and Nagasaki. World War II ends.

IN THAILAND	IN THE WORLD
1992 Election of General Suchinda Kraprayoon; mass demonstrations force him out of power; civilian rule returns.	
1997 Currency crisis plunges Thailand and its neighbors into severe economic trouble.	**1997** Hong Kong is returned to China.
2001 Elections won by Thaksin Shinawatra of new TRT party.	**2001** Terrorists crash planes into New York, Washington D.C., and Pennsylvania.
	2003 War in Iraq begins.
2004 Hundreds die as a result of Islamic insurgent attacks in the southern provinces. The Indian Ocean tsunami in December kills almost 10,000 people in the south of the country.	**2004** Eleven Asian countries are hit by giant tsunami, killing at least 225,000 people.
	2005 Hurricane Katrina devastates the Gulf Coast of the United States.
2006 Thaksin Shinawatra is ousted in a bloodless coup. Retired general Surayud Chulanont is appointed interim prime minister.	
2007 General elections held in December	
2008 Return to civilian rule. Abhisit Vejjajiva is elected prime minister as the head of a new coalition.	**2008** Earthquake in Sichuan, China, kills 67,000 people.
2009 Violence continues in the southern provinces, with more protests on the streets of Bangkok.	**2009** Outbreak of flu virus H1N1 around the world
2010 A long-running border dispute with Cambodia leads to fighting between Thai and Cambodian forces.	**2011** Twin earthquake and tsunami disasters strike northeast Japan, leaving more than 14,000 dead and thousands more missing.

GLOSSARY

bot (boht)
The largest building in a temple compound, used for prayer and ordination.

chedi (CHAY-dee)
A spirelike devotional monument.

jai rohn (jai rohn)
A "hot heart." Anger, impatience, and visible displeasure are examples of *jai rohn*.

jai yen (jai yen)
A "cool heart." To have *jai yen* is to stay calm in all situations.

karma
The effect of one's thoughts and actions on his or her position in society and the next life.

krathong (kra-TOHNG)
A floating devotional lamp.

krengjai (KREN-jai)
A show of consideration for the feelings of others in a social situation.

Muay Thai
Thai kickboxing.

muban (MOO-bahn)
A cluster of houses; a village.

Negrito
Indigenous peoples of Africa, the Philippines, the Malay Peninsula, the Andaman Islands, and South India. Negrito peoples are usually small in size and have dark skin.

pha sin (pah sin)
The traditional costume Thai women wore before the 19th century. A Thai woman wore her *pha sin* as she would a wraparound sarong.

sanuk (sah-NOOK)
Amusement, enjoyment.

Tai
The generic term for the groups of people related to Thai. The Tai migrated from China to Southeast Asia around 2,000 years ago.

tambon (TAM-bohn)
A group of 10-15 *muban*.

tam boon (tahm boon)
Making merit. Acts of *tam boon* can improve a person's status in society.

Thammasat
Rules of behavior that kings of Sukhothai followed. The kings had to be forthright, gentle, merciful, and pious and never angry, violent, or vindictive. They also had to give alms and put the welfare of the citizens above their own.

viharn (vee-HAHN)
Temple compound building used for rituals.

wai (weye)
A greeting sign. Thai *wai* by raising both hands, palms joined, to lightly touch the body between the chest and the forehead.

FOR FURTHER INFORMATION

BOOKS

Campbell, B., Frances Hawker; and Sunantha Phusomsai. *Buddhism in Thailand* (Families & Their Faiths). New York: Crabtree Publishing Company, 2009.

Clayton, T. *Thailand* (Changing Face of ...). London: Hodder Wayland, 2005.

Cooper, Robert. *Thailand* (Culture Shock!). London: Marshall Cavendish, 2009.

Murdoch Books. *The Food of Thailand: A Journey for Food Lovers* (Food of the World). Sydney: Murdoch Books, 2005.

Phillips, D.A., and Charles F. Gritzner. *Thailand* (Modern World Nations). New York: Chelsea House Publishers, 2007.

Phra, Peter Pannapadipo. *Little Angels: The Real Life Stories of Thai Novice Monks*. London: Arrow Books, 2005.

Thoennes, K. *Thailand* (Countries of the World). Cessnock, Australia: Lioncrest, 2006.

DVDS/FILMS

Amazing Thailand. TravelVideoStore.com, 2005.

Bustling Bangkok. TravelVideoStore.com, 2010.

Cities of the World: Bangkok, Thailand. TravelVideoStore.com, 2009.

Cosmos Global Documentaries: Siam, a Glorious Kingdom of the Past—Thailand. TravelVideoStore.com, 2004.

Isan: Folk and Pop Music of Northeast Thailand. Sublime Frequencies, 2004.

Paradise on Earth: Phuket, Thailand The Complete Travel Guide to Phuket, Thailand. TravelVideoStore.com, 2005.

MUSIC

Classical Music of Thailand. World Music Library, 1994.

Music from Thailand and Laos. Arc Music, 2000.

Taste of Thailand. Bar de Lune, 2007.

Thailand: Ceremonial and Court Music. Music Earth, 1998.

BIBLIOGRAPHY

BOOKS

Cooper, Robert and Nanthapa Cooper. *Thailand* (Culture Shock!). Singapore: Times Editions, 1990.

Forbes, Andrew and David Henley. *Khon Muang: People and Principalities of North Thailand*. Chiang Mai, Thailand: Teak House, 1997.

Goodman, Jim. *Thailand: Land of Enchantment*. Singapore: Times Editions, 1996.

Guelden, Marlane. *Thailand: Into the Spirit World*. Bangkok: Asia Books, 1995.

Hoskin, John. *Bangkok*. Singapore: Times Editions, 1990.

Kekulo, L. Bruce. *Wildlife in the Kingdom of Thailand*. Bangkok: Asia Books, 1999.

Landon, Margaret. *Anna and the King of Siam*. New York: Harper and Row, 1944.

Mulder, Niels. *Inside Thai Society*. Chiang Mai, Thailand: Silkworm, 2000.

Phongpaichit, Pasuk and Chris Baker. *Thailand's Crisis*. Chiang Mai, Thailand: Silkworm, 2000.

Rabinowitz, Alan. *Chasing the Dragon's Tail*. New York: Doubleday Anchor, 1992.

WEBSITES

Bumblehood: Literature of Thailand. www.bumblehood.com/article/wuWq8-XvSiiYjxdy_mACmQ

CIA—the World Factbook: Thailand. https://www.cia.gov/library/publications/the-world-factbook/geos/th.html

ClimateTemp.info: Thailand. www.climatetemp.info/thailand/

Joshua Project: Kui, Kuay, Suei of Thailand. www.joshuaproject.net/people-profile.php?rop3=200120&rog3=TH

Khamer Logue. http://khamerlogue.wordpress.com/2010/12/08/khmer-as-%E2%80%98invisible-minority%E2%80%99-language-ethnicity-and-cultural-politics-in-north-eastern-thailand/

Ministry of Foreign Affairs, Thailand. www.mfa.go.th

One Stop Chiang Mai: Golden Triangle Tourist Guide. www.1stopchiangmai.com/northern_thailand/golden_triangle

Royal Thai Government. www.thaigov.go.th/webold/index-thai.htm

Thailand Environment Institute. www.tei.or.th/main.htm

Tourism Authority of Thailand. www.tourismthailand.org/

U.S. Department of State: Thailand. www.state.gov/r/pa/ei/bgn/2814.htm

Wild Watch Thailand. www.wildwatchthailand.com

World Wildlife Fund Thailand. www.wwfthai.org/en/

INDEX

INDEX